W9-ASX-398

Conversations with Miller

Mel Gussow has written the three previous volumes in this series, *Conversations with Pinter*, *Conversations with Stoppard* and *Conversations with and about Beckett*. He is also the author of the biography, *Edward Albee: a Singular Journey*, and is the co-editor of the Library of America's two-volume edition of the plays of Tennessee Williams.

His other books include *Theatre on the Edge: New Visions, New Voices*, a collection of theatre reviews and essays; and *Don't Say Yes Until I Finish Talking: A Biography of Darryl F. Zanuck*. He has written profiles for *The New Yorker* and other magazines.

As a longtime drama critic for *The New York Times*, Mel Gussow was a winner of the prestigious George Jean Nathan Award for Dramatic Criticism and a recipient of the Margo Jones Medal in 2002. He is currently a cultural writer for the same paper.

By the same author

Edward Albee: A Singular Journey

Theatre on the Edge: New Visions, New Voices

Conversations with Pinter

Conversations with Stoppard

Conversations with and about Beckett

Mel Gussow

Conversations with Miller

APPLAUSE
THEATRE & CINEMA BOOKS

for Ann

Conversations with Miller
By Mel Gussow
Copyright © 2002 Mel Gussow

Library of Congress Cataloging-in-Publication Data

Gussow, Mel.
  Conversations with Miller / Mel Gussow.
     p. cm.
  Includes index.
  ISBN 1-55783-596-9
  1. Miller, Arthur, 1915---Interviews. 2. Dramatists, American--20th century--Interviews. 3. Playwriting. I. Miller, Arthur, 1915- II. Title.
  PS3525.I5156 Z687 2002
  812'.52--dc21   2002007688

  ISBN: 1-55783-596-9   Printed in Canada

APPLAUSE THEATRE & CINEMA BOOKS
151 West 46th Street
New York, NY 10036
Phone: 212-575-9265
Fax: 646-562-5852
Email: info@applausepub.com
Internet: www.applausepub.com

SALES AND DISTRIBUTION:

NORTH AMERICA:

HAL LEONARD CORP.
7777 West Bluemound Road
P.O. Box 13819
Milwaukee, WI 53213
Phone: 414-774-3630
Fax: 414-774-3259
email: halinfo@halleonard.com
internet: www.halleonard.com

Contents

Introduction

Once when I asked Arthur Miller what he thought his legacy would be, he answered without hesitation: "Some good parts for actors." He explained that when actors and directors decide to do his plays it is not because the plays have "great moral importance" or "even literary importance." It is the challenge of the role, for example, the many different ways an actor could approach Willy Loman. Gradually he allowed that there was, of course, another level to the question, that there was more to be seen in the plays, that they deal "with essential dilemmas of what it means to be human." Then he made it clear that they were always intended to be generic as well as specific.

As he said, he could not have written *The Crucible* simply because he wanted to write a play about blacklisting — or about the Salem witch hunts. The center of the play is "the guilt of John Proctor and the working out of that guilt," and it exemplifies the "guilt of man in general." In other words, there is a moral as well as social and political base to his work, and it is that sense of morality, of conscience, that distinguishes him from other important playwrights.

Miller is one of four major American playwrights of the twentieth century, the others being Eugene O'Neill, Tennessee Williams, and Edward Albee. O'Neill began as the pioneer experimentalist; his principal contribution was in his depiction of the disparity between reality and illusion. Williams was the great poet of our theatre, while Albee, with searing intensity, probes marriage, family, and the failure of the American dream. Miller's individual significance is for his moral force and his confirmed sense of justice, or, rather, his sense of correcting injustice wherever he finds it — in business, art, politics, the courts, the court of public opinion. He does this in his life as well as in his plays. Through PEN and other

organizations, he has been an outspoken advocate in protect-
ing civil liberties and helping to free dissidents – and also in
fighting censorship.

His plays, especially *Death of a Salesman* and *The Crucible,*
continue to speak to theatregoers around the world, in China
and Russia as well as on home ground. They are unified by
recurrent themes and motifs: embattled fathers and sons;
fraternal love and rivalry; the price that people pay for the
choices they make in life; the cost of ambition, compromise,
and cowardice; suicide as sacrifice; the loss of faith. Perhaps
above all, the plays are about the law, in Miller's words, as a
"metaphor for the moral order of man."

It is no coincidence that lawyers figure prominently as
characters in almost all his plays: Alfieri in *A View from the
Bridge*; Quentin, Miller's surrogate and the protagonist of
After the Fall; Bernard in *Death of a Salesman,* the young man
who is arguing a case before the Supreme Court and does not
need to tell Willy — or anyone — about it. Interestingly,
Bernard is one of the characters that is closest to Miller
himself. In a sense, Miller is lawyer as playwright, aware of all
sides of a dispute but clear about where he stands: for an
essential moral truth.

Were his plays only works of social consciousness, they
might have faded along with the plays of Clifford Odets. In
play after play, he holds man responsible for his — and for his
neighbor's — actions. Each play is a drama of accountability.
Watching *All My Sons,* it is impossible not to be aware of
contemporary parallels — of accidents in nuclear plants, of
defective tires and cars being shielded by the companies that
produce them, of drug manufacturers who put products on the
market before they have been adequately tested. There are
other through-lines in his art; for example, the theme of power
and the loss of power. In *The Crucible,* power rests with public
opinion and the judges who run the system, but also with the
individuals who first cry witch. The author is searching for an
ultimate authority that will eventually rectify wrongs.

In Miller's plays, man loses his confidence, his position, or,
like John Proctor, he loses his good name. How does he
behave, how will he react? Can the character gain — or regain

— the courage to go on, or will he find solace in embracing defeat? Willy Loman is confronted by a loss of faith, a loss of pride, and an end to possibilities. He has always thought that if he works hard and is a good salesman he will succeed, and that his sons will succeed after him. It turns out that this is a dream based on false values. For Willy, as for Miller, the Great Depression was a turning point, in itself the end of an American vision of prosperity. The second great public event in Miller's life was the Washington witch hunt, conducted by Senator Joseph McCarthy and the House Un-American Activities Committee. This signaled the blinding of an American vision of individual freedom.

After O'Neill, the American theatre was dominated for many years by Williams and Miller. *A Streetcar Named Desire* in 1947 and, two years later, *Death of a Salesman,* were revelatory occasions. As we know, they are not only great plays but paradigms of two extraordinary careers, and both were directed by Elia Kazan. For Williams, his move from his home in St. Louis to New Orleans, where he found new freedoms, changed his life and inspired his art. For Miller, the University of Michigan offered a somewhat related experience. It was there in an academic environment, away from his home in New York, that he began writing plays and expanding his vision.

It would be easy to think of Williams and Miller as opposites, Williams as a hauntingly autobiographical playwright who could transform his dreams into plays that probed the human heart; Miller as more of an objectifier, a kind of American Ibsen. In Harold Clurman's analysis, Ibsen had "a compelling force to combat meanness, outworn modes of thought and hypocrisy," and was "in quest of a binding unity, a dominant truth." However, as Clurman added about Ibsen, his plays are also "deeply autobiographical...dramatizations of his emotional, spiritual, social and intellectual life," and it is that quality that gives his plays their "staying power." All these things can be said equally about Miller.

Miller is as admiring of Strindberg as he is of Ibsen. Even as he is aware of — and offended by — Strindberg's misogyny, there is another side to Strindberg with which

Miller can identity: Strindberg's "vision of the inexorability of the tragic circumstance, that once something is in motion, nothing can stop it," that, as with the Greeks, it is impossible to avoid the power of Fate. Miller also expresses an admiration of and a compassion for Williams. Instead of rivalry, there was a sense that the success of each fed the other and that, in tandem, they elevated Broadway. The kinship is also personal. As Miller said, "Tennessee felt that his redemption lay in writing. I feel the same way. That's when you're most alive."

When Miller is not writing plays, he spends time building tables and other furniture. He loves carpentry and often uses it as a metaphor for playwriting; the objective is to build a better table, to write a better play. In one of our conversations, I suggested that he had already made a terrific table – *Death of a Salesman* – very early in his career and wondered, after that, what the incentive was. He said first of all that *Death of a Salesman* was his tenth play and added that each play has a different aim. A different wood? No, "same wood" – the Miller wood, firm, solid, like mahogany, seemingly impervious to the weather (but perhaps not so impervious to critics). The same wood, but a "different aim — to create a different truth," and for Miller each play becomes "an amazing new adventure." Some playwrights write the same play over and over again: not Miller.

As he has said, "I have a feeling my plays are my character and your character is your fate." Ineluctably, he is drawn to his study, where he writes far more intuitively than one might suppose, an artist sustained not only by his ideas but by his moments of inspiration. He also said, "There's an intensification of feeling when you create a play that doesn't exist anywhere else. It's a way of spiritually living. There's a pleasure there that doesn't exist in real life — and you can be all those other people."

Several years ago, Miller was in Valdez, Alaska to receive a playwriting award at the Last Frontier Theatre Conference. While he was there, he and a local official went fishing for salmon in Prince William Sound, which is surrounded by a glacier. As they passed an iceberg, Miller's companion leaned over the side of the boat, chopped off pieces of ice and brought them aboard. Miller touched glacial ice. "Eight million year-old ice," he said in astonishment. "It doesn't melt."

When I was in Valdez for that same conference a few years later, I too touched glacial ice — and thought about Arthur Miller. When he told me that story, I suggested that if ice can last that long, perhaps that says something about the survival of civilization and of art. Never one to sidestep a metaphor, he said, "You hang around long enough...you don't melt."

Miller is very much a survivor, an artist who has gone his own way without regard for fashion or expectation. There are more plays and adventures to come. The work, at its best, is both timely and timeless, which is why the plays continue to be done.

And there are also some good parts for actors.

I first met Miller in 1963, when *After the Fall* began rehearsals as the first production of the Lincoln Center Repertory Theatre. After that, our meetings were brief and sporadic until 1984, when I wrote a profile of Dustin Hoffman for *The New York Times Magazine*. At the time, Hoffman was acting in *Death of a Salesman,* and I followed the show from Chicago to Washington, D.C. to Broadway, speaking to Miller along the way. In 1986 I brought Miller together at the *Times* with Athol Fugard, David Mamet, and Wallace Shawn for a panel focusing on playwrights and politics. Statements from that panel are included in this book. Late that year and into 1987, Miller and I had a series of conversations, excerpts of which were used in an article that appeared in the Arts and Leisure section of the *Times.* The most recent conversations have not been published before.

Occasionally, over the years I have also seen Miller in more informal circumstances. At one point, his daughter Rebecca temporarily moved into an apartment in our building in Greenwich Village, and one day, like any helpful father, Miller carried suitcases and other possessions up the staircase. One other thing must be said about him. For those who do not know him, he presents an austere, Lincolnesque image. Actually, he is down to earth and congenial; he likes to tell stories and can be wryly amusing.

At the end of October 2000 I was a participant at an 85th birthday celebration of Miller at the University of Michigan. This was an international symposium entitled "Arthur Miller's America: Theatre and Culture in a Century of Change." Because Miller had an accident and suffered a cracked rib, he did not attend, but he did a live television interview from his home in Connecticut with Enoch Brater, the director of the symposium. There were several days of panel discussions and speeches dealing with his plays, his autobiography, *Timebends,* and various film and opera adaptations. Many of these events were academic but all of them revealed the intensity and the depth of the interest in his work. I spoke about Miller and his legacy in the American theatre.

After my talk, there were questions from the audience. I realized that there were several people in the house, experts on Miller, who were, coincidentally, experts on Samuel Beckett, and that I had shared many panels with them on that subject. I wondered if there was any connection between Miller and Beckett. A surprisingly lively discussion followed, as we agreed that despite their obvious disparities (of style, of subject matter), there was a certain kinship in their political awareness and social conscience. While Miller does not share Beckett's pessimism, they stand on common ground in terms of their idealism. In my conversations with Miller, it has also been clear that he has gradually come around to an appreciation of Beckett's contribution as a playwright. Miller once artfully characterized *Waiting for Godot* as "vaudeville at the edge of a cliff." As a writer, Miller is himself more experimental and less naturalistic than his public image.

There is another point of commonality: the two are tall, thin, stalwart, great-looking men. I don't think either one has ever taken a bad photograph (of course, Miller has his own personal photographer, his wife Inge Morath). Beckett and Miller never met, but if they had, what would they have talked about? Women? "No," came the correct answer from the audience. Probably each would have been far too discreet (although Beckett might have been interested in knowing about Marilyn Monroe). Perhaps they would have talked about the cause of human rights, about politics, or their fondness for clowns and comedians.

In contrast to Harold Pinter and Tom Stoppard and, certainly, to Beckett — the subjects of my previous *Conversation* books — Miller has written widely about his own work; he also wrote his autobiography. There is no shortage of Miller commentary. What the *Conversation* books have in common (besides a major playwright as subject) is that each is written from a single point of view over an extended period of time and there is an arc to the conversations. With Miller, my first impression was of a man with a certain emotional detachment from his plays and the events of his life. I soon realized that he is someone passionately committed to his work and his political and social beliefs. At the same time, he has maintained an ironic perspective on his own success and a residual faith in the possibilities of the art form that he has chosen to practice.

On September 11, 2001, as terrorists attacked the World Trade Center, Arthur Miller and his wife were in Paris. They had flown over at the invitation of the French government, co-sponsors this year of Japan's Praemium Imperiale, a $125,000 award that was to be given to Miller in October. On that morning, a friend of Ms. Morath had called them from Germany to tell them the news. Naturally they turned on the television. Two weeks later when I telephoned Miller at his home, he said about the attack, "I could not absorb it while it was happening. It still is incomprehensible. It's all terrible. What can I say?"

Then he added, "From the news reports, it seems that the Bush administration has given up talking about a massive air strike. I have an idea. Maybe we should send over a fleet of bombers and drop 10,000 pounds of food on them" — meaning the Afghans.

Through the rest of 2001, while Miller — along with everyone else — was trying to come to terms with the terrorism and other acts of violence around the world, he found himself immersed in the busiest of seasons. A movie of his 1945 novel *Focus* was released and received respectful reviews and Richard Eyre began rehearsals for his Broadway revival of *The Crucible* (starring Liam Neeson and Laura Linney).

In January 2002, Miller and I met for lunch, and I gave him a copy of the British edition of this book. Asked if he might consider writing a sequel to his autobiography *Timebends*, he said he would rather spend his time writing plays. He had finished a new play, *Resurrection Blues*, which he had been working on for several years. It is about a rebel leader who is captured by the government and sentenced to death. Plans were underway for David Esbjornson to direct the premiere at the Tyrone Guthrie Theatre in Minneapolis that summer, perhaps followed by a Broadway production. Miller said that going through his papers he had also come across a one-act that he had written in the 1950s. It had never been performed. He said it was "about two old farts in a hospital." Reading it as if it were a new play, he said that he liked it and might authorize a production.

He had had dinner the previous evening with Eyre, and expressed his enthusiasm about the revival of *The Crucible*. Yes, he said with a laugh, the production was top heavy with 20 producers, and they all came to the first day of rehearsal. He recalled that when the play first opened on Broadway in 1953, it had one producer, Kermit Bloomgarden. He spoke about the decline of Broadway, once a place of great hope.

The Man Who Had All the Luck, his first Broadway play — and a failure that closed after four performances — had been revived the previous summer at the Williamstown Theatre Festival and the Roundabout Theatre Company was bringing it to Broadway in the spring. This meant that Miller would have two major revivals on at the same time.

It was a most convivial lunch. What Miller did not say was that his wife Inge was very ill. She died at the end of the month. On April 26, there was a memorial for her at the Mitzi Newhouse Theatre at Lincoln Center. Honor Moore, Zoe Caldwell, and other friends spoke about her and her work as a photographer. Then Miller talked, beginning with a moving story about Inge's flight from Berlin at the end of World War II.

14

Because she refused to support the Nazis, she had been forced to work in an airplane factory in Berlin, along with prisoners of war. With the war over, she left the factory and began walking, planning to return to Vienna, where her parents had been living. On her journey, she was befriended by a soldier who had lost a leg in battle. With his help, they scavenged for food and found an occasional ride on trucks. Finally — presumably weeks later and her clothes in tatters — they arrived in Vienna. In shock, she was unable to remember where the family home was, and the soldier led her to the working class section of the city. No, she said, they lived in a grand house. They walked across the city and in a more prosperous neighborhood, she recognized a door. That's their house, she said, and knocked on the door. Her mother answered and, in astonishment, said, "How did you find us?" "He led me," Inge said, but when she turned around there was no one there.

Miller said that to this day he did not know if anyone had accompanied Inge on her journey or if she had imagined the stranger. There was something magical about his wife, he said. Then he talked about her life and the closeness of their long marriage. She was, he said, "a noble woman." Contradicting the perception by some critics of him as a prosaic figure, Miller spoke with eloquence and deep emotion

This book begins with a conversation from 2001, then flashes back to 1963.

MEL GUSSOW
May 2002

15

Conversations
with Miller

"I'm rewriting *Hamlet*"

On a rainy, windswept day, I met Miller at his apartment on the East Side of Manhattan and we walked several blocks to the Cinema 70 café, where he had his favorite lunch, a turkey club sandwich. The following Monday he was giving a speech at the John F. Kennedy Center in Washington, as part of a series of lectures sponsored by the National Endowment for the Humanities. The title of the talk was "On Politics and the Art of Acting," and our conversation began with that subject.

AM: I'm going to talk about Bush, Gore, Clinton, Roosevelt, and several others as performers. Roosevelt was probably the greatest performer we ever had as President. One of the best in our time was Reagan, who, without thinking about it, perfected the Stanislavsky method by making a complete fusion of his performance with his personality. He didn't even know he was acting.

MG: Sometimes he would talk about his personal experiences and it would turn out that they would be scenes from movies in which he had acted.

AM: He couldn't tell the difference between what happened in the movies and what he did.

MG: And he acted better as President than he ever did on screen.

AM: He was perfect for it. On the other hand, in Bush's campaign for President, every time he approached the podium, he would give a furtive glance left and right, as though he were an impostor. What the body language tells us! There's a story that Bobby Lewis [Robert Lewis, the director and teacher and one of the founders of the Actors Studio] used to tell. When he was a very young actor, he was an assistant to Jacob Ben-Ami, who was a famous Yiddish actor. It must have been in the late 1920s and Ben-Ami was in a play downtown [Tolstoy's *The Living Corpse*]. One scene in it became the thing to see. Ben-Ami stood on the stage with a gun to his head for many minutes, trying to get up the courage to shoot himself. Finally, with the tension at its peak, he lowers the gun. He can't do it. It was sensational, because people really thought he might blow his brains out. Bobby watched that every night from the wings. He asked Ben-Ami, "How do you do that?" Ben-Ami said, "I can't tell you now, because it will get out and it will ruin my performance. At the end of the run maybe I'll tell you." The run ended and Bobby said, "Well, you promised to tell me." He said, "My problem in acting that scene is that I'm absolutely not suicidal. I can't imagine the circumstance in which I would take my life. So how could I ever approach how this man must be feeling? I thought, where am I trying to do something, and I can't do it? It's when I'm about to jump into a cold shower. So what am I doing up there? I'm trying to take a shower." [*laughs*]

So in my speech, I say, which is the one we're voting for: the guy who is seen with the gun to his head or the guy taking the cold shower? What I'm saying in effect is that acting comes with the territory. When you walk out of your house to face the world, you begin to act a little bit.

MG: Your point is that we all play roles?

AM: Sure. Where's the everlasting truth? It's only in art — when the artist approaches the paper or the canvas. Tolstoy said that we look in a work of art for a revelation of the soul of the artist. For an artist to put his soul in a work of art, he can't act. It has to be for real. Characteristically, in all ages, the artist has the hardest time.

MG: In one of our earlier talks, you said that Tennessee Williams said his redemption lay in his art, and that you agreed with him.

AM: Absolutely. And the one good thing about growing older

— or old — is that art literally is the only thing that endures out of an age. When I think of the few plays that have endured and the millions of speeches and exhortations that have disappeared. I can't remember the authors. I can't remember the pieces.

MG: There are a few speeches that have lasted: Martin Luther King's "I have a dream," Roosevelt's Pearl Harbor radio broadcast.

AM: That's a form of art, though...

MG: And in some cases the speaker didn't write it.

AM: Roosevelt didn't. He had Bob Sherwood [Robert E. Sherwood] write it.

MG: A playwright.

AM: Whatever doesn't turn into art vanishes. What have we got of Rome or Greece or Assyria — some carved stones done by sculptors, some poems scribbled on papyrus?

MG: What about the horror of the Taliban destroying those Buddhist statues?

AM: Isn't that something! You know, the Chinese revolutionaries in the 1960s did that. They attacked temples and destroyed a lot of art in China.

MG: To take it a step further, what about societies that destroy the artist? I'm thinking of the House Un-American Activities Committee and the blacklist.

AM: The way I put it: art is civilization's revenge on people who think the artist is just this idiot who doesn't know how to tie his shoes. Art is the one reassurance that I have about the continuity of the human race.

MG: Does the artist have an obligation to write about political events?

AM: I can't speak of obligations in relation to art because if the artist doesn't naturally feel what he or she is doing, the thing is not going to work. But I have to say that the great challenges in the past were the challenges of the society's

21

mal-direction. Whether you look at all the Greek plays or at Shakespeare, they were very politicized stories. The most important art we've got comes out of such confrontations. You're eschewing the source of great energy if you think that art is purely a conversation with yourself, which is what it became in many cases. But we've still got people who know this. There's always an attempt on the part of Phil Roth or Robert Stone or Don DeLillo, a number of very good writers who are trying to grapple with this monster that we're all being devoured by.

MG: You're naming novelists, not playwrights.

AM: I think most of the playwrights of any seriousness know that the challenge is to bring the great beast down. Like Tony Kushner, who wrote the big play that dealt with Roy Cohn, *Angels in America*. I'm sure he's still at it. He's devoted to that kind of reality.

MG: That's one thing that keeps you going as a writer.

AM: Yes. Trying to bring order to this chaos, which is next to impossible.

MG: How is your new play going?

AM: I've got two of them I'm working on at the same time. One of them is half finished.

MG: *Resurrection Blues*?

AM: I wrote one version of it, but I want to look at it again. I let it lie for a while. There's something not right about it. There's wonderful stuff in it. The form of it is cracked somewhere.

MG: Cracked?

AM: Split, somehow. It's a good cartoon for the play, in painting terms. I've got to change some of the colors in it.

MG: What's the other play?

AM: The other play is about an old man, not me, who is nearly blind. He's pursued by his life and he's trying to get out of it. It keeps tackling him again and again.

MG: Trying to get out of it by suicide?

AM: No, no, not suicide, not at all. He's trying to outlive it. It's got a lot of different scenes, but it's basically taking place in a house out in the country.

MG: And it's not about you.

AM: I couldn't be the way this guy is. He's a former builder of tract houses, a hundred houses at a time. The usual business-man whose desire was to be a poet, or an actor. I think I'll be able to finish that play soon.

MG: I just read *The Man Who Had All the Luck* [which failed on Broadway, in 1944].

AM: They're doing it in Williamstown this summer. Scott Ellis is directing it. They did a reading at the Roundabout Theatre down on 23rd Street. I said, I'm not sure the damn thing is going to work. They cast it gorgeously. Then Scott said, "Can I do it in Williamstown?" I said, "Certainly — with these people." They're all excited about it. There really is nothing like it, for good or ill. It's basically the story of a young man, who for reasons he could never put his finger on, always succeeds. The point comes where he becomes more and more certain that anything he's managed to accumulate, including his family, will be struck down by retribution from some source.

MG: Was that something you felt at the time?

AM: That was based on someone I knew about in the Midwest, a man who hung himself. He couldn't stand the tension. I guess it reflected the fact I already had a great leveling instinct.

MG: What do you mean by leveling instinct?

AM: That no one, including me, should ever regard himself or be regarded as being more important than anybody else, nor be paid more or be given more homage.

MG: The original story was told to you by your first wife's mother?

AM: Yes. I knew the wife in the story slightly. I never met the man. He was dead by that time. It was my interpretation of what had happened to him. At an extremely young age he was a very successful businessman. He ended up owning a half dozen different businesses and became paranoid. He couldn't have been more than 27, 28 years old. He was certain that he would be robbed, that people were going to set fire to various things. He was a farmer, among other things, and he ended up hanging himself in his barn.

MG: That's not how the play ends.

AM: I had not written it with the kind of total darkness that it would require. I couldn't hang him with this play. In any case, he came very close to saving himself, and had he had a little better help he might have survived it. I never believed in the end of that play. Years ago, I rewrote the last three or four pages. I couldn't find the requisite kind of ambiguity that was necessary because it's an impossible philosophical situation. The play is basically trying to weigh how much of our lives is a result of our character and how much is a result of our destiny. There's no possibility for me to come down on one side or the other. And I was not able to until I reread it again. I didn't want it done with the other ending.

MG: You've said that the play is "the obverse of the Book of Job." The central character believes that man experiences at least one bad thing in his life — and he keeps waiting for that one thing to happen.

AM: That's right. He's waiting for that blow. Subsequently I thought that a lot of people feel that way.

MG: You don't feel that way, do you?

AM: I used to, more than now.

MG: After you first began to succeed?

AM: Even earlier. Everybody I knew had faced a calamity, and some had survived it and some hadn't. The idea was that no one could go through life unscarred.

MG: This is one of the themes of Albee's *The Play about the Baby*, that man has to experience tragedy in order to be human.

AM: I haven't seen the play yet, but I think there's truth in that.

MG: Have you faced your calamity?

AM: [*laughs*] Eight or ten times! I came to the edge of life a number of times, once with the House Un-American Activities Committee. Then with my divorce. I was married seventeen years. That was a big blow, that I would come to that.

MG: And Marilyn too?

AM: Marilyn. After all, we were married for five years [1956-1961]. She never lived that many years with anybody else because nobody could hang in there that long. I wasn't writing anything in those days. I would call it a calamity — to me. It was for her, too, I suppose, but she was more accustomed to it. Her life as a whole was full of calamity.

MG: The woman who had no luck — even though she became a movie star.

AM: That whole story of the movie star and the way it consumes people — it's so banal by now. And it gets repeated again and again and again. You pick up a paper and this loving couple are suddenly at each other's throats. It's the oldest story. Success is the great man-eater. Surviving it is as hard as attaining it, if not harder. Early on I fastened my arm to the idea of the theatre, specifically tragic theatre, as a root that goes back to the beginning of time. By attaching myself to it, I felt safe. I could always revert to it, in worse times. Maybe I could add to it somehow.

MG: If you hadn't found that?

AM: I don't know what would have happened.

MG: After *The Man Who Had All the Luck* failed, you were thinking of doing something else, like writing fiction.

AM: Yes. The play closed in four days and was totally unremarked. I promptly said, I don't belong in this and I wrote a novel, *Focus*, to start off my career as a novelist. The idea of spending all that time — and hope — on something that could be wiped out in a matter of days. By the way, *Focus* has been made as a film, with Bill [William H.] Macy. At the time of *The Man Who Had All the Luck*, I had hardly been close to the theatre. When I saw the play, I couldn't recognize anything about it as something that I had written. It seemed utterly strange and alien. It wasn't the failure of the play that sent me into writing a novel. It was the fact that I had no connection with what I saw on stage.

MG: Meaning they did it wrong?

AM: I'm not sure they did it wrong. Maybe there was no way to do it. They didn't try to trivialize it or cheapen it in any way. Joe Fields was the director — the brother of Dorothy Fields, and I think his father or grandfather was Fields of Weber and Fields [the vaudeville comedians]. He walked around with books of French poetry in his pocket, and he wrote the crudest Broadway farces. He adored the play but he didn't know how to do it, and I didn't know any more than he did. I thought I should write novels because I didn't think I could realize my work on stage. I decided I would never write another play.

But at some point, early on, I began thinking of myself as a playwright — with no evidence. My role, or my identity, was that of a playwright. I couldn't identify myself as a novelist. I lived in a country with no theatre. But that identity never left me. Now when I sit down and think about writing and think, oh where am I going to put this play, what I am going to do with it if I write it? — it's an absurd question. Somewhere, somehow, some place will do it. Maybe some guy out in Chicago will do it.

MG: Then you heard the story that became *All My Sons*. Both those plays were based on overheard stories.

AM: Correct. As a matter of fact, now that you say that, both of them came from the same woman, my ex mother-in-law, who was probably the least dramatic human being ever born. She had absolutely flat Ohio speech, without emphasis of any kind. She was a Catholic who simply accepted life as a disaster, the way some people did in those days, hoping for a better one in the afterlife. They lived to die. That was what was called religion.

MG: And she told you the two stories.

AM: And she dropped two stories on me.

MG: What if she hadn't?

AM: I probably would have found something else. Your antennae are out there catching all these flies. Some you eat and some you don't.

MG: All you need is a good fly?

AM: The right kind of fly, you go with it. I start plays all the time, and drop them because they don't work. That's a very common thing with me.

MG: Many plays unwritten or half written.

AM: Or just started. I started to do something just as sort of a joke about six months ago — I'm rewriting *Hamlet*. That the truth of the play is that his father never died, that the so-called uncle is his father, the king is really alive. That's why they say, what is the matter with him, what's got into that boy? If you look at that play, except for that first scene, nobody else sees or hears that ghost but him. The only time it starts to get real for him is when he discovers that he stabbed the old man — through a curtain, of all things. This is all a reverie of a seventeen-year-old boy.

MG: As you say that, Shakespeare is turning over in his grave.

AM: [*laughs*] If you look at the lines of the people talking to him, it's as though they are wondering, what got into his head? And indeed he knows a hawk from a handsaw. The dream quality of the whole thing, and the youthful quality are essential. That scene talking to his actors, cooking up his performance — it's right out of hallucination. I didn't finish it. I never will. But I had a good time for about two days, piecing it together.

MG: How did you come to start it?

AM: I was reading *Hamlet* two years ago and what struck me powerfully was the surprise in the voices of the other people. Practically everybody is trying to figure out what he's talking about.

MG: Some director probably could stage it that way.

AM: Yes, but the Hamlet would have to be, or appear to be seventeen. I don't know if it's ever been done that way.

✳

MG: In an essay, you said that perhaps you should have written *The Crucible* as farce, that that was the only way to handle the subject.

AM: Well, when you consider that Ring Lardner Jr. sat in front of that committee and six months later he was in prison with one of the members of the committee [J. Parnell Thomas]. That's out of French farce.

MG: To you it was tragedy.

AM: At that time it seemed like tragedy, and indeed it was. I was just thinking this morning about [Robert] Hanssen who has been caught as a spy. Nobody would think now of electrocuting him, although he could be. Remember [Aldrich H.] Ames who gave away the whole naval code so that the Russians knew where every ship was and what the ships were talking about to each other. He got 20 or 25 years. Because if you spy for money, it's less alarming than if you do it for an idea. I think with all of them there is a feeling of infinite power. They are sitting there with their counterparts: there are two people. One of them is the real guy and the other guy is the fellow who is stepping into the cold shower, who is controlling the whole situation. It's a kind of revenge. "You think you got me as your subject, you go on thinking that, because I'm controlling you." In the case of Ames, he was making 40 or 50 thousand a year. He had a Jaguar and a Ferrari, a house in Mexico, another one — and nobody wondered about it! You've got to really be desensitized somehow to not have questioned this.

MG: You asked for your FBI files under the Freedom of Information Act.

AM: I did, and there's nothing there. It's all blacked out. What you get is newspaper clippings. There was one thing which they forgot to black out, but it's meaningless anyway. They reported I had a dinner party at my house in Brooklyn Heights and clearly from the report they had followed one of my guests home. Imagine the manpower. It's like the Stasi in Germany where they had approximately half the population spying on the other half. God almighty, what an age! We deserved a Shakespeare, but we didn't get one. The roaring conflicts! I feel now that the 1950s really did emasculate the culture, more than one is willing to confront. Not just the radicals. There weren't that many anyway. But in general it set up a warning flag, a very profound one, to watch your step. It was more effective because it wasn't overt. So it was very deep, psychologically speaking. The whole theatre turned into our version of the absurd, which was on the whole far less political than European theatre. Ionesco wrote plays that were pretty sharp.

MG: You and Tennessee were thriving in the 1950s on Broadway.

AM: Yes. But one got the feeling even then that there was a high pressure on the whole situation. I'll never forget one afternoon I had to be at my lawyer's office to sign some papers. Another lawyer, Eddie Costikyan, was brought in as a witness to my signature. In passing, I said, "The whole Broadway scene is corrupt. It's corrupt because money rules everything." Money always ruled, but there were exceptions. There were crazy people like Billy Rose who would back [Clifford] Odets, and never expect to get his money back because Odets's plays didn't run that long. [Kermit] Bloomgarden when he started, Bob Whitehead, five or six in that whole gang. And now it's just been bogged down by money people and investors who have no connection with the art. And Costikyan said, "That's a communist position." I'll never forget that. Imagine! He was, I suppose, a liberal man. That's what I mean by the flag going up. Uh-oh!

MG: And you survived that, too.

AM: Yes. But I was depressed. No end to it. I never thought I would feel this way again, but they're going to bring on a cultural crisis. It may be that's what they want, in the belief that the majority of the American people will be with them.

MG: Last October I was in Ann Arbor for your 85th birthday celebration at the University of Michigan. Because of your accident, you were not there.

AM: I was in Norwich, England, and there was a broken sidewalk right along by the cathedral, and I was looking up at something in the cathedral, and I tripped on my left foot. I went down like a tree. [*hits the table*] Oh God, the pain. Interestingly, the doctor said, "This will be all right in three and a half weeks." I said, "Why a half?" He said, "That's how long it takes." I got back here, went to my doctor. He said, "It will be all right in three and a half weeks" — and it was. I said, "It's about the only thing you guys can predict." He said, "That's right."

MG: That was the first time I was in Ann Arbor.

AM: Back in the 1920s, Ann Arbor was the place where all the radicals who were thrown out of other universities ended up, from Harvard, Yale, Princeton. They had a terrific faculty. They were radicals not necessarily for political reasons. One famous guy was thrown out of Harvard for advocating birth control.

MG: Your time at Michigan meant a great deal to you, didn't it?

AM: It was the greatest thing, it was the luckiest thing I could have done. There was, and still is, an atmosphere in that place, of democracy, in the best sense. It's full of the voices of all kinds of people. In those days and today, they had a large number of Asian students, which you didn't find in other places. And Arabs. In those days, Columbia, Yale, Harvard, it was all lily white. Wearing white buckskin shoes. The teach-ins originated at Michigan.

MG: And that's where you became a playwright. It was a turning point.

AM: I don't know what would have happened if I had not gone there. In those days, there were very few, if any, creative writing courses. Forget playwriting. Colleges didn't think that was a serious affair, so to find a school that was interested in playwriting was really very, very unusual. That was terrific for me. I also had one teacher who taught the essay. I got a lot out of that. One day he said, "Miller, I want to see you. Let's go for a walk." The idea of going for a walk with a professor was quite unusual. We walked and he said, "You know, you could be a professional essayist. I think in about eight or ten years." Eight or ten years? I couldn't wait eight or ten months!

October 24, 1963

"That man up there isn't me"

It was the first day of rehearsal of After the Fall, *Miller's first new play to open in New York since* A View from the Bridge *in 1955.* After the Fall *also marked the beginning of Lincoln Center, New York's major venue for the performing arts, and of the Lincoln Center Repertory Theatre, under the leadership of Elia Kazan and Robert Whitehead. While construction was taking place on the site on Manhattan's Upper West Side, the play was to be staged in a temporary theatre downtown in Washington Square.*

Kazan had directed Miller's first Broadway successes, All My Sons *and* Death of a Salesman, *but there had been a break between the playwright and director after Kazan had testified as a friendly witness before the House Un-American Activities Committee. As Miller was to write in his memoir,* Timebends, *Kazan's testimony "had disserved both himself and the cause of freedom." Now the two were working together again — on a play that dealt partly with that era, the Red witch hunts of the 1950s. One of the two principal characters in the play was a self-destructive film star based on Marilyn Monroe, Miller's second wife. Just as Miller was finishing the play, Monroe died, apparently from an overdose of sleeping pills. All these events were in the air; so much was at stake in terms of the playwright's reputation and the future of Lincoln Center.*

Before the rehearsal began (in a Manhattan ballroom), Miller said, "The play is about a lawyer in New York today. The form is extremely free and very subtle. It's a gathering of connections. It's the happiest work I've ever written, and by that I don't mean it's funny." In response to the suggestion that it was drawn from his life, he said, "All my plays are autobiographical," and added unconvincingly, "This less so."

33

Miller, Kazan, Whitehead, and Harold Clurman, the literary adviser of the repertory company, sat at a table. Kazan was in his shirtsleeves, the other three were in jackets and ties. They faced the actors in the company, who included Jason Robards and Barbara Loden (in the leading roles of Quentin and Maggie), Faye Dunaway, and Hal Holbrook. In photographs of the event, I can be seen in the back row, covering the rehearsal for Newsweek *magazine. Television newsmen were also in attendance.*

Kazan said, "This is the first rehearsal of the Repertory Company of Lincoln Center. In a moment, Arthur Miller will read you his play, After the Fall." *Holding a script, Miller began, "The action takes place in the mind, thought, and memory of Quentin." He stopped there and said, "That's all I'm going to read." Those of us who were outsiders were asked to leave, and then Miller returned to the reading, which, with a break for dinner, went on into the evening.*

Some weeks later when the cast had moved into the ANTA Washington Square Theatre, I met Miller for the first time — on the set of After the Fall, *a sparse arrangement of modular units. Miller was in a particularly relaxed mood. He was reclining on a block that represented the marital bed of Quentin and Maggie. Leaning back, with his hands clasped behind his head, he looked like a man at peace with himself and his past.*

After the Fall *did not live up to expectations, partly because Maggie was so close to the image of Marilyn Monroe without delving deeply into her character and the relationship between her and Miller (or his surrogate in the play). Quentin, a lawyer not an artist, also remained at a distance, proof that the playwright believed it when he said, "That man up there isn't me."*

Encouraged by his associates at Lincoln Center, he followed After the Fall *with* Incident at Vichy, *his first exploration of the Holocaust. Clurman directed it at the Vivian Beaumont, the new Lincoln Center theatre.*

In 1972, Miller had written what was ostensibly his first

comedy, The Creation of the World and Other Business, *his version of the Book of Genesis, with Adam and Eve as the principal characters. The composer Stanley Silverman had written several songs for the show, and then asked Miller if he would be interested in collaborating on a musical version. Gradually the two began adapting the show into* Up from Paradise. *On April 18, 1974, we met at a rehearsal, and Miller talked about the origins of the production.*

AM: Students at the University of Michigan were going to do scenes from a play of mine that had never been performed. Then they started fiddling with this and they thought they would do it on an experimental basis. As soon as we started musicalizing it, the whole form began to change. It became possible to use narration and dialogue, a kind of statement and response. There was a whole new spirit. Stanley started writing more music to words I had written, and we backed into it. Before you know it, we were rehearsing ten hours a day.

MG: In working on the musical, have you been able to clarify the play?

AM: It's more clearly what I intended in the first place: a metaphor for the ingestion of God by man. Man ingests God and replaces him, taking over his function. He destroys God on stage, and one second later, he resurrects him in his memory. Adam is God on earth. He accepts his humanity rather than remaining a perpetual child of innocence. The form is right for this kind of myth. I'm writing in condensed verse instead of with a linear psychological build. One can present rather than represent. With the original we never arrived at a satisfactory production. Everything was done psychologically.

MG: Could you compare the play and the musical?

AM: I love the abruptness of the changes that take place. The play has been steered by thematic necessity. All the actors will be on stage watching the whole thing instead of vanishing into a realistic set. It's a kind of joyful playfulness rather than any deadly realistic attitude. There

35

was no stylistic unity in the original. Once we were off on the wrong foot it was impossible to get back on the right foot. This time we got started in the spirit of the play. Willy-nilly it came about, a sort of improvisation from day to day — on a very organized basis. The actors have enormous freedom. One doesn't have an investment or the whole pressure of opening in New York hanging over one's head. We will play Michigan and another college. It could take two years from one university to another.

MG: But don't you want to prove something about the play's failure on Broadway?

AM: I don't have to prove it on Broadway. For years, I've said we're making a big mistake by failing to attempt to organize audiences in the country. At the University of Michigan, there is a tremendous physical plant. Costs are minimal. What makes this really feasible is that the actors are young and willing to move around. I've had more genuine creative enjoyment doing this than I've had in many years. It's enormously stimulating to work on a kind of ad hoc basis. Everybody's pores are open. Theatrical illusions come from language and sound and use of bodies rather than the use of scenery. Everything on stage is conditional — open all the time. In the morning we throw these kids a whole new curve, and they leap to it. Twenty minutes, and it's in!

MG: How does it feel to be writing lyrics?

AM: It's my first time. I love to do it. I started out as a singer. I had my own radio program in Brooklyn when I was fifteen. I sang pop songs, great songs of the 1930s. I was accompanied by a blind pianist. I think we had about eleven people listening. I never got paid. Once I listened to what I was singing and I got embarrassed. I realized there were some damn good singers walking around without work.

MG: You're going to be the narrator of the musical?

AM: My doing it made it more of an event.

Miller and I spoke occasionally during the next decade. The Archbishop's Ceiling, a play about art and politics, was scheduled to open in December 1976 at the Long Wharf Theatre in New Haven. In August, the playwright summarized the theme as "what the soul does under the impact of immense power, how it makes accommodations and how it transcends the power." The scene is a room in an unnamed Communist country, the residence of a former archbishop. There are five characters, one of them an American writer.

AM: The ceiling symbolizes what happens below.

MG: It sounds like an overtly political play.

AM: We aren't always aware that we are making adjustments to social power. The play is political in that sense, but it's not a tract. Some people thought *The Crucible* was a tract-like play against McCarthyism. That was not my intention. I don't believe in analogies. But it's not just a crazy situation in a far-off place. It could happen in a corporation boardroom — anywhere unbridled power is immense.

MG: Is there humor in the play?

AM: Well, I think so! But it's a drama obviously. Certainly it's not a comedy — except to God. It's a big laugh — up there. Down here, it's quite serious.

A View from the Bridge *had been revived at the Long Wharf Theatre in New Haven in 1981, in a production starring Tony Lo Bianco as Eddie Carbone, and it would move to Broadway in February 1983. In October 1982, Miller was at Long Wharf directing two of his one-acts,* Elegy for a Lady *and* Some Kind of Love Story.

MG: What provoked you to direct your one-acts?

AM: I wrote *Elegy* a year ago. I finished *Love Story* a few months ago. Both share an attitude: they walk the jagged edge of unreality. In *Elegy*, a man is trying to discern his relationship to a woman he thinks is dying. She isn't on stage. The other is a crime story of a private investigator who has a relationship with a woman who he is sure has the truth to a murder case. She is a bit mad. Both are departures for me. I despaired of explaining them to a director, so I'm directing. In February I'm directing *Salesman* at the Beijing People's Theatre. I'll have a guy [Yin Ro Chang] absolutely fluent in English alongside me. I wondered about their ability to handle time shifts. They feel they could do it. It centers on the family, which is an obsession of the Chinese.

MG: Besides *A View from the Bridge,* is there any other play of yours you would like to see back on Broadway?

AM: I'd like to see all of them back. But Broadway is a less giving environment than it used to be. It's a surreal Coney Island, a big calliope making a lot of noise. Broadway will come back. It always does.

February 17, 1984

"It was just an image I had of this feisty little guy who was taking on the whole world"

In 1984, Dustin Hoffman played Willy Loman in a revival of Death of a Salesman *on Broadway, directed by Michael Rudman, and with John Malkovich and Stephen Lang playing Willy's sons. I followed the show from Chicago to Washington, D.C. to New York and wrote a profile of Hoffman for* The New York Times Magazine. *Before flying to Chicago to see the play and talk to Hoffman, I had lunch with Miller in New York.*

MG: I remember more than fifteen years ago talking to you about Dustin. You said he would be a very interesting Willy.

AM: Dustin has great internal life on stage, and he has a quality of sympathy. He can deal with more than one feeling at the same time. For my work, that's very important. Lee Cobb at his best does what Dustin does at his best — with many fingers on the instrument. Dustin can play contradictions, and not just straight lines. He is what I call an integral actor. He really does have to know with his brain and his belly what the center of a dramatic issue is. He can't work from the perimeter. I find this exhilarating because he peels it off like an onion until he gets to the middle of the middle of the middle. That can drive somebody crazy who is not accustomed to such assiduousness. There's no harder worker than that man. I'm now an old geezer. I have never seen anybody attack anything with such thorough, total dedication. I shouldn't say "nobody;" there have been actors that do, actors that I've worked with, but he is among the most rigorous of such people.

MG: Who are the others?

AM: Lee Cobb was led to it by Kazan because he could also get a little lazy. He had a marvelous voice and looked great. He could always lean on his equipment to get him through narrow spaces. Dustin can't.

The waitress comes over and he orders a turkey club sandwich, but asks her if they could eliminate one slice of bread. She hesitates and says, "I'll tell them to." "Tell them to," says Miller, "and that will be the greatest thing they can do all day."

Dustin starts to turn on a motor that doesn't stop, day or night. He doesn't sleep much when he's working, running around in his running shoes, keeping himself fit. It's a real athletic contest. I find it terrific — that kind of dedication.

MG: What's in him that allows him to play Willy?

AM: I think it's his own psychological makeup. I'm only guessing: his relation to his own ego and his own father, which he talks about on the stage sometimes, as an illustration of what he's up to. That helps, if you've got some image like that.

MG: Does he actually relate his father to Willy?

AM: To a degree, I think. There is also another element which is completely superficial. When I originally wrote the play, I conceived of Willy as a small man, with a large wife. For this production, I had to change one line back to the original. Willy at one point says, "People don't seem to take to me. I'm not noticed." With Lee Cobb, I made it: "I'm fat. I'm foolish to look at. I didn't tell you but last Christmas I was calling on F. H. Stewart's and some salesman went by and said something about "walrus," and I cracked him." The original line, which is what Dustin is saying is, "I'm small," and instead of "walrus," it's "shrimp."

For the first production, we tried to find a small actor, but we ran out of them; they weren't right for it, temperamentally. We considered some very good actors: Bud Bohnen [Roman Bohnen], who was with the Group Theatre and is long since dead now; and Ernest Truex.

MG: Why did you think of the character as small?

AM: I don't know. It was just an image I had of this feisty little guy who was taking on the whole world. It was Kazan who finally came to me and said, "Well, I've got an actor who can do it, but he's certainly not small." And it was Lee.

MG: In the years since, the role has generally been played by large men, like George C. Scott.

AM: It usually ends up with somebody who is like Lee. Thomas Mitchell was a big man. When I talked to Dustin, he had that kind of feisty quickness that I always associated with Willy. You see, Willy is changing direction, like a sailboat in the middle of a lake, with winds blowing in all directions, and I associated that with a small man rather than with a great big man who makes slower turns. Willy's a sidestepper. He's a little puncher. And that of course is what Dustin always appeared to be to me.

MG: In the light of previous productions, it sounds like a re-interpretation.

AM: Right. It is. He's a cocky little guy sometimes, and overwhelmed by the size of the world.

MG: Does that change the play?

AM: Yes. I think it does, to a degree. Probably in one sense it has a different kind of tragic effect, if you want to call it that. He's striving to climb to the top of the mountain, and the striving is perhaps clearer in this kind of production. He doesn't have it natively given to him by life. He's got to struggle for it. For example, his whole relationship to his sons — he says, "I thank almighty God, you're both built like Adonises." That has a slightly different meaning when one son is John Malkovich, close to six feet, and the other one, Stephen Lang, is a real strong guy, a very powerful fellow. Suddenly something else comes off the stage.

MG: Whereas Cobb physically dominated his sons.

AM: It's a slightly different weighting.

MG: Cobb was younger when he played it, but he always seemed to be a father, where Dustin has always been a son.

AM: Dustin has made such a vivid impact in what he has done that people associate him with those roles. I have no problem with it. I don't think the audience does either. And it's not just his makeup. He does behave like Willy. I don't think for a moment about him being too young, which, of course, he isn't. Or being a son and not a father. Willy is 63. As you said, Dustin is seven or eight years older than Lee was. Lee had natural advantages in that direction. Lee was born old. He was lugubrious, depressed. Dustin has always been chipper, full of energy. One of the surprises has been how little he needed to do to appear to be that old. He started off way older. I said, "Look, you're being 75."

MG: When the idea was first presented to you, you didn't greet it with surprise.

AM: No. I first met Dustin when Ulu Grosbard was doing that production of *A View from the Bridge* down in Sheridan Square [in 1965]. Dustin was the stage manager. Bob Duvall was playing Eddie. Dustin had not done any work that I had ever seen. It was Ulu who said, "There's a guy here who should play Willy Loman." I looked around [at Duvall and Jon Voight, who was also in the cast] and I said, "I don't see him. Where is he?" He pointed at Dustin, and Dustin in those days looked like he had just barely gotten out of high school. Ulu saw something there. Of course he had known Dustin as an actor, which I had not. Maybe it's some fix on the high intensity of that part. Personally I doubt that anybody over 50 could do it without some difficulty. You have to be a theatrically naive man, such as I was, to have thought you could do this unrelieved role, and find actors for it. You have to have young vigorous people to play it.

MG: Going back to *A View from the Bridge,* I would suppose that neither you nor Ulu would have thought of Dustin, then or today, for Eddie Carbone.

AM: No. And maybe there's the ethnic thing too. But I'm sure he could play him.

MG: Willy has to prove himself again and again. That's a strong line in Dustin's work.

AM: Of course, Dustin is always doing that as an actor. He's always taking on new challenges. And each of these challenges seems more improbable than the other. [*laughs*]

MG: What do you play after you play *Tootsie*? You play Willy Loman?

AM: Right. When he told me two years ago he was going to play a woman, I really was floored. I had no notion what this was all about. But as soon as he showed me the photographs of tests that he was making, about makeup, hairdos — he was already investigating feminine types. It wasn't simply, how do I look? He was being a specific type of woman, spiritually, psychologically. Then I thought, if he's going to do that, I suppose it could work. He wasn't doing it like *Charley's Aunt*.

Inge [Morath, Miller's wife, the photographer] has a photograph, which I think is prescient. She took it during the phonograph recording with Lee Cobb. Dustin, sitting next to Lee, was playing Bernard on the record. He was holding a tennis racket — and watching Cobb. I don't know what he was saying, but it was a typical Lee Cobb frown of a monumental disaster. It was obviously not while he was acting. He was just discussing something, and you can see Dustin watching him like a hawk. It's such a telling moment. You can see him just watching him, saying, how is he doing this?

MG: When did this current production begin?

AM: It started about five years ago. We went on casting for months. Every once in a while Dustin would say, "Do you think I could really do it?" The closer he got to the mountain, the more scared he became, as he should be. I never had very much doubt once he broached it seriously because his way of working is the way I like to try to write. It's an integrated way of working. The consistency of the character, as between page 6 and page 60, was deep in his mind: he draws it all in, rather than playing one moment after another.

MG: Did he have an image of the character before he began?

AM: He had a general image. I kept telling him, this is the hardest job you'll ever try to do. In six months from now, you're going to call me up and say, you know I think I'm getting to understand what I have to do. But he's exhilarated. I give him notes at night, as the director does.

MG: What do you say in the notes?

AM: He's too angry at one point, too caustic, or vice versa, he isn't sharp enough with somebody. He's moving into a scene in the past without having the blues. He's miraculous. He'll get up onstage the next day and you see a complete shift. Another actor will tell you, well, I'll get it next week, by which time, you've forgotten what you said. He will attempt anything that is viscerally connected to the character, with the story, with the relationship.

MG: Has he ever done anything wildly wrong — and then it's been thrown out?

AM: Not that it's wrong, but a different way. It's a purely interpretative thing. He might be moved to tears at one point — and he shouldn't be weeping, he should be seeing something clearly. One of the hardest things to do is the yin and the yang at the same time. As Dustin puts it, when the dancer leaps in the air, the lower part of his body is trying to stay on the earth. That stretch is what you want. Try doing that. You've got to be a little lucky to do that. He'll try it.

MG: Does that remind you of any other actor?

AM: The closest I've come to that kind of approach was not an actor, it was a director, and that was Kazan. Dustin is now just right. He has the maturity for Willy Loman. Thank God we didn't try to do it too long ago. In my opinion, actors past a certain age — it differs with each actor — are going to get tired. This is running a 15 K race. This is not a 100-

yard dash. Act one is an hour and six or seven minutes. It's a full-size evening. You've got to be in shape. He keeps himself in shape, as if he's going into a boxing ring.

MG: When he went into the role he was already trying to dress and think like Willy.

AM: He bought himself a 1940s-type hat, trousers, trying to feel what it felt like to wear those kind of clothes. I guess he was working himself into how Willy stands and walks, and, of course, clothes can make a difference. He's wearing double-breasted suits. As Dustin Hoffman, he certainly wouldn't do that. And how shabby it should be, how ill-pressed or how pressed — he's a meticulous worker, every detail is considered and made real. It reminds me of Olivier. When we were casting, Dustin read with everybody every day. He was there all day.

MG: Were the casting stories true, how he thought about the possibility of G. Gordon Liddy playing Willy's brother Ben?

AM: Oh, yes. That's how he cooked up Gordon Liddy. He wanted to see what somebody looked like who goes into the jungle. We normally would have cast the play in weeks. This one went on for months. He kept saying we've got to look at everybody. We had open calls [auditions open to everyone]. We have two women in the play who came in out of open calls, and one of them is extraordinary.

MG: What about Liddy?

AM: He came in and read the part. You associate him with such danger: he's a gunman. I cannot imagine him being able to play a role and ever escape that identification. Ben is supposed to be a bit of a larcenist. He's fooling around with Biff and suddenly Biff's on the floor, and he doesn't know what hit him. In this production Ben's got a sword cane. The guy in the original production was an over-the-hill opera singer, Tom Chalmers, a baritone with the Metropolitan Opera. This time it's Louis Zorich. Dustin wanted to know what this guy was like in reality, somebody who would be the colonialist and walk into a jungle, and come out rich. He was being Willy in all situations. We would have actresses come and be the woman in Boston. He played a whole scene with each one, to see what a different kind of woman she was. Also Miss Forsythe. There are all kinds of Miss Forsythes. She can be a dumb broad, she can be super sophisticated. Her background is never explained; it's implied.

MG: What about the sons?

AM: We ran through a lot of Happys. At least two were superb.

MG: How does Malkovich compare to Arthur Kennedy, the original Biff?

AM: In 1949, nobody would act like Malkovich. Arthur Kennedy came on with a kind of extroverted energy that was his own, the character's, and the style of the time. This is pre-Brando, pre-James Dean, before actors thought of emotion as coming off an inner cool. Malkovich is of a different school completely, but very effective.

MG: Could Brando have played the role?

AM: Sure, it could have easily been him. And in fact if you think of him in *Streetcar*, his extroversion in *Streetcar* was in contrast to that moody introverted vitality that we later identified with him. Malkovich is more introverted, more private.

MG: And Stephen Lang?

AM: That's Happy. The more sincere he gets, the more humorously unbelievable. He has an incredible physical life.

MG: Kate Reid as Linda Loman?

AM: She's got tremendous power.

MG: She's not too old for Dustin?

AM: I was worried about that. I don't think so. When they come on stage, they both seem to be very profoundly married. If you go too young, then it makes Dustin younger.

MG: Didn't you find yourself losing your patience when the casting took so long?

AM: Yes, I never like casting. I hate it because I have to meet all the actors and shake their hands at the end and then I just get pained at the idea of having not to hire them, especially when they're good actors and they're just not right or someone else is better. That's one of the reasons I've stayed away from directing. I just can't face it every morning. You have to come in and look at 25 actors and know at a glance that quite likely some of these people are not going to work.

MG: Rudman was hired as the director because you had seen his London production of *Salesman*?

AM: Pure and simple. He had done that and they had paid my fare so I went over. I had grave doubts that they could ever pull it off, with the accent and all the rest of it. Warren Mitchell was extraordinary. Michael showed a grasp of the play in talking to him later. Dustin also happened to have seen that production. I think that this may have given him a little kick because Warren Mitchell — I don't know how old he is, but he can't be older than Dustin. When he was cast as Willy Loman, the British press thought it was a joke. But he won every acting award. Dustin called me from London after I got back — he didn't know I had been there — to tell me how excited he was about the play. He's been fixed on it for many years.

MG: He often talks about his return to the stage. Just about every two years he talks about *Hamlet*.

AM: After this, I would hold my breath. He might well be able to pull that off.

MG: Does he have the voice?

AM: Well, he'd get it! For example, Lee Cobb had to leave the production in less than four months, I think, because he couldn't speak anymore. Lee had a big baritone voice, which he misused. There's a certain amount of yelling that you have to be careful about. Cobb was in the Group Theatre. He was a Stanislavsky actor. He knew all about using your voice, but he didn't bother with it. He also smoked cigars. I guess that didn't help. We had a specialist there all the time trying to keep his vocal cords from being destroyed. And I warned Dustin early on. When we started rehearsing, I heard that shout. I went over to him and said, "Look, kid, nobody can do this — and yell. You'll be out of gas." He went to a doctor. At the moment he's still a little bit hoarse, but I suppose that's always going to be the case. I can hear it immediately when he walks on stage, if he's doing it right or not. He's got to get his voice down there [*lowers his voice*] so he can use it. I don't think he's ever had a part that required this much talking at an intense level. Almost every scene he's in starts like that! You can't do that for very long. He works at it. He doesn't let it slide. He's not a procrastinator like most of us are. If there's a problem, he goes after it. He'd be a great military commander. He'd laugh if I ever said that, but he attends to details and never forgets the objective.

MG: Maybe he could do Patton as well as Willy Loman. How would you compare George C. Scott [who directed and starred in a revival of the play on Broadway] to Dustin?

AM: Scott was very much closer to Lee. He had tremendous power. As I told him, I don't believe an actor ought to direct himself. There's simply too much to do in that part to be directing that play. Only somebody with the iron constitution of George Scott would attempt it. I don't believe in that way of working. Olivier did it with Marilyn in *The Prince and the Showgirl*, and it didn't work. The picture would have been immeasurably better with a good English director.

MG: In a movie there is more to worry about.

AM: There's plenty to worry about in this play. The detail in this thing — it really swamps the mind. It reminds me of trying to do a full-blown production of one of the Elizabethan plays. Suddenly you've got a whole new gang of characters on the stage. Take the restaurant scene. There are two women who have got to come on, a waiter, a different atmosphere completely, a whole new mood. All the stuff you've been doing up till then — forget it. You're in a new situation.

MG: If you were writing the play today, you probably wouldn't allow yourself to do that.

AM: Probably not. Very often I look at it and I say, what a heroic idea — not in the moral sense — but in the aesthetic sense. And I think of Tennessee's work. We had a different idea of the theatre. I think it changed somewhere around Beckett's entrance. With Beckett the emphasis was on the intensified incident.

MG: Two or three characters in an intense situation.

AM: Yes. With us, it's a tapestry, the whole story, with all the details, with a beginning, a middle and an end. So how could anybody want to act it and direct it at the same time?

MG: What's the range of people who have played Willy? You directed it in China.

AM: I have a book coming out called *Salesman in Beijing*, which was my log or diary of that production. That guy in China was a Dustin guy, now that I think of it. He's about Dustin's size, but stockier, wider. He came to the end of each night and looked at me and said, "This is quite a job." He's a wonderful actor, a very literate guy who speaks perfect English. He said, there's one part of this character I can't quite link up to because our societies are so different — that Willy is so proud of these great stores that he dealt with. He said, in China, in the scale of Confucian values, the merchant is at the bottom, and no merchant would put his own family name, for example, on his business. He would call it the Grocery Store of the First Happiness. They never want to be involved in trade. He said, "I'm trying to find some similarity in China of this idea you have of the salesman going forth into the darkness to conquer the enemy."

Up until the First World War, or earlier, there were goods

trains moving from Beijing out into the country, and they had been protected by horsemen whose job it was to escort those trains against bandits. When the railroads came in, their services were no longer necessary. They ended up in county fairs doing tricks with guns, a little bit like Annie Oakley and Wild Bill Hickok, and they could talk with romantic nostalgia about that past.

MG: How did you feel about Fredric March in the movie of *Salesman*?

AM: He had been our first choice for the play, but he was in a movie at the time. I don't think he understood the script. A lot of people didn't. He would have been terrific on stage. But I think that movie [of *Salesman*] was misdirected and misconceived. They made Willy into a psycopathic case. It was symptomatic of the 1950s to try to take off any criticism of the system. Instead of using Willy as representing something, he represented nothing but Willy. The consequence was that Freddy was simply playing Dr. Jekyll and Mr. Hyde again. A little loony, pathetic. It was a great disappointment to me. They also cut out parts of the play that were too inflammatory, not just about the system but about relations between people. They made them milder. They feared any kind of fire. They blanded it out.

The integration of that play is, if I must say so, total. I wouldn't know where to set a break. It's a real weave of my own preoccupations. It's a web of being that's got a structure — I can't tamper with it. I wouldn't know how to do it. We're going to do a television film of this production. I'm going to see that it stays right there.

MG: You're not going to put Willy in a car, as they did with Fredric March in the movie.

AM: I knew that was an error, but I didn't know why. I just felt it was impossible. I know now why. The play's not a realistic play. It's Willy's obsession and all the voices in it are various voices. This is taking place in his head. You know my first title was *The Inside of His Head*. It's only as years went by that I realized that's a subtitle. They're all moving around inside of his head.

MG: And your original idea for the set was a cranium?

AM: Yes. The first set that I wanted — not seriously, because I couldn't imagine how you could do it — was a concave cranium. This is a better set, I must say.

MG: On screen and on stage, Dustin has always played naturalistic comedies or dramas.

AM: What he's had to do in this one, I guess, is to combine that sense of a documented social type with the inner dynamics of this poem, which is what it is. They did a production at the Tyrone Guthrie Theatre [in Minneapolis]. The Cronyns played it [Hume Cronyn as Willy, Jessica Tandy as Linda]. Guthrie didn't know the play. He turned to me and said, "They all say this is a realistic piece. This is a poem for eight voices." Therefore, to take it out and suddenly document it with automobiles, highways — it simply violates the thing. It's part dream, and the hermetic nature must never be broken, no matter what medium you're going to use. The Swedes did *Salesman* three years ago. Bo Widerberg, who did *Elvira Madigan*, made the same mistake. It was to give it soulful documentation. You can't do that.

MG: Is that a problem with Dustin?

AM: He's trying to do something better. He's making it absolutely recognizable in every detail, the right handkerchief, everything the way it should be. He's not just playing the naturalistic side, which can easily be done. You can reduce the whole thing. This has been his major, basic preoccupation.

MG: Is Willy necessarily more Jewish in this production?

AM: Well, Lee was as Jewish as Dustin. Maybe more, because Dustin comes from a different generation. I don't know. You'd have to ask somebody else about that. I never noticed it.

MG: I felt that more in the London production with Warren

Mitchell.

AM: Well, he was trying to do that. The whole thing is absurd to me because it's played everywhere in the world, and this is not a consideration. I guess Lee was the only Jew in the first production. That was just the way it worked out. The same thing here with Dustin. I never discussed that with him. He's playing his father's generation. But in truth, such is the calendar that his father would have been a son of Willy. It's the wrong generation. I met his father and I was surprised to see that he was born after some of the stuff that I remember.

MG: Did his father remind you at all of Willy Loman? Or of your father?

AM: Well, in a way. Any guy who sells; they have a certain forward motion. They're making it, and they love it! It reminds me about Willy's love of business. The love of worrying about these selling problems, supply, demand. Businessmen who are successful are all in love with their work. Willy adores it.

MG: Even when it kicks him in the face.

AM: In the deepest sense it's a game. You don't play tennis well, but you keep coming back to it for another game. You never envision yourself really being a great tennis player, or golfer, or runner. There's something about playing it — it's acting. Salesmen are actors. They devise strategies in performance. In China, it occurred to me: I thought this whole thing is about an actor, and when I wrote it I knew very few actors. The moment when the actor is not in demand anymore.

MG: And you play a role you don't want to play.

AM: Playing for others.

MG: Has this production taught you anything new about the play?

AM: I don't think so. I directed it myself in China and to direct it in another language you really have to translate it. So I had been through it last May. I think I circumnavigated that play pretty well. As a cultural artifact what they make of it is quite interesting.

MG: Dustin has often based his characters on real people in his life. In playing Willy, was he perhaps thinking of you?

AM: No, he thinks of me more like Charlie [the neighbor]. I'm more unflappable than Willy, although when I read it to him, when I give him line readings, he loves that. He says, "That's the way it sounds!" But I don't think it's my character. He wouldn't be able to make use of that, I don't think. Too much of life is inside. It's not outside.

MG: You wouldn't want to play Willy?

AM: No. I don't want to play anything.

MG: It's been a long time since Dustin's done something that's firmly scripted and established.

AM: He loves that about it. He says, "Imagine, we don't have to change anything."

MG: Doesn't he want to?

AM: Oh, no. He loves the discipline of that text. He plays upon it. He relies upon it. It's hard to think of limits for him. He's a fanatic, gets his teeth into something and makes it yield. He'll create a new Willy. It ain't going to be the other one.

MG: It won't be yours?

AM: It's Willy. It's just different than any Willy I've seen.

MG: Certainly the shortest.

AM: That's right. It makes the dream bigger, somehow, the fact that he's grappling with this tremendous force, the society. He's plucky; there's a certain pluckiness in the character because he has so few advantages in relation to the struggle.

MG: He has charm and the smile.

AM: Dustin is charming. They adore him. The imprint of a star like that is engraved deep in the mind. He's been in disguise a lot. Maybe that helps. Maybe the audience is not as amazed as one would imagine. There's no question in mind that he has drawn so far a far younger audience than we would normally expect to see for any play, any straight play, certainly any play about an old man. You don't expect to see them pouring out of colleges and high schools. They do for him.

MG: Does that encourage you to bring back *The Crucible*?

AM: *The Crucible* is done a lot more than *Salesman*. With *Salesman*, it's a naive audience in the sense that there's a tremendous energy in that audience. When there's laughter there are blocks of it. When they're shocked, you can hear them gasp. When Willy loses his job, they groan. It's a real surprise. It's very visceral. They're more alive to it. Older people sit there: what else is new? If we succeed, it may be the most important thing it accomplishes, to bring in a new audience. In Chicago, I would say every night there are at least a half dozen people who look to me to be 20 years of age standing outside with a handwritten sign, "I want to buy one ticket."

MG: Cobb left the theatre and then came back years later to do Lear — and he couldn't do it.

AM: He left *Salesman* and became a sheriff on a horse. You can't be a sheriff on a horse and then suddenly do *King Lear*. It's a rigorous art, if you're going to do it well.

MG: Dustin hasn't tuned his instrument for the stage for all those years.

AM: Well, he's having to tune it now. He picked one now. He needs an orchestra up there. Every night he comes off shaking his head: "Jeez I didn't do that thing right." I say, "Well do it right tomorrow," and he says, "Now I lost the other one." Trying to hold that whole thing. And he's a perfectionist. If it's almost good, it's more excruciating than if he missed it altogether.

The next day I flew to Chicago and went to the matinee of Death of a Salesman. *Afterwards I went backstage. On the door of Dustin's dressing room there was a sign that said "Dave Singleman," the man who died "the death of a salesman, in his green velvet slippers in the smoker of the New York, New Haven and Hartford." After Dustin showered, we were driven back to his hotel where we talked about Miller and* Salesman.

MG: How much is Willy your father?

DH: I started off thinking it was all my father. That's all I had to draw upon. I think it's the first play I ever read. I have a book of American plays edited by John Gassner that my brother gave me in 1954 when I was in high school. *Death of a Salesman* was the first play in the book. I was seventeen and it just knocked me out. And my father was a salesman, and to me it was my family. If anybody, I was Happy, trying to stop fights by clowning around. The relationship between my brother and my father had a lot of similarities, in terms of the emotional struggle.

My father was a representative of wholesale furniture that factories made. He had swatches, pictures of dining room sets and he would try to sell to the retailers. He got fired in his sixties — they didn't need him any more — literally by saying, "Don't come in."

Lisa [Hoffman's wife] says that when she watches the play she sees a lot of Arthur mixed in with my father. I hung around with Arthur almost daily since last June. When you study the play and hang around with him, you hear the rhythm. He says a lot of the same words in the play. He says, "Isn't that remarkable?"

MG: You don't try to mimic Arthur's voice.

DH: No, I tried to do him, but I couldn't. I don't know who the voice is. That just came out. It's not my father either. The way he deals with me I deal with the sons a lot. He's very physical.

He suddenly realized it was after six and it was time to go back to the theatre for the evening performance. We continued the conversation at breakfast the next day.

DH: Willy was a friend of Arthur's father. Linda came from a higher stock. She married down. He's knocked her down. In the first act, when he says, shut up, she shuts up. My father did that to my mother constantly. The story in my house: in those days, fathers didn't bring up the children. They made the money. My father would come home and hear that there was a fight, that my brother and I were driving my mother crazy. He'd say, "When I have to come into this, you guys better watch out." In other words, when I have to start being a father, that means there's trouble. He'd always use these images. "I'll take your goddamn heads and smack them together," or "I'll take a strap." I was five years old. These images would scare the shit out of me.

My father wasn't a loser. He was a successful travelling salesman, but I don't think he was successful in his own eyes. He had his truisms that I believe in and try to do in my work: "Give them more than they paid for" and "Get the work done first."

MG: Miller says you've been talking about doing Willy for about five years.

DH: The day I got married in Roxbury [where Miller also lives], I woke up in the morning and went for a run and went past this house. I later learned it was the house where *Salesman* was written. Arthur's a first rate carpenter. He has a big workshop, where he makes tables and chairs. He built this house with his own hands when he was thirty-two and he went in and wrote *Salesman*. He said he would look out and say, "Tell me what to say, Willy?" He said the play just came; he doesn't know how it happened.

Arthur came over to my house and I said, "I'd like to do a play." He said, "You don't want to do *Salesman*, do you?"

56

I said, "Why not? I just don't want to do it now. I'm too young." We started talking. I said, "I just want to know what you think." We read the play aloud to Arthur. Lisa read Linda and I did my father as Willy. I said, "Is that him?" He said, "Certain things." My first anchor was my father, then the more I hung around with Arthur, it was Arthur.

I listened to Cobb do it on the record. I hadn't listened to it since we had cut it. And it depressed me. I thought I can't do it. I recalled all the times I had watched him. To see him do Willy Loman was like watching Rodin. This fucking piece of sculpture.

MG: How do you wipe out that memory?

DH: First I tried, tried, to imitate it; let me see if I can be as good. Then I realized I couldn't. I'm not Cobb. I don't have his kind of power. I don't have those guns. In a way that was a liberating thing. It took me a long time to realize that what I was going toward was the opposite. Instead of this walrus, I was going to be this spitfire. Willy Loman is an amalgam of things that Arthur wrote. Partially it's one guy that his father knew, partially his father and partially himself. The more you get to know Arthur, you see Arthur in every character that's in that play.

January 17, 1986

"To be a playwright... you have to be an alligator. You have to be able to take a whack and be able to swallow bicycles and digest them"

At my invitation, four playwrights — Arthur Miller, Athol Fugard, David Mamet, and Wallace Shawn — met at The New York Times *for a symposium on playwriting. The discussion ranged widely, but focused on several questions. How are playwrights affected by world events? Can art and politics co-exist in the theatre? From what sources do playwrights draw their inspiration? What is the future of a theatre confronted by increasing economic pressures? Although all agreed that there is no strong public demand for plays dealing with political and social issues, they were unanimous in feeling that this was their primary calling. A common concern about the escalating cost of theatrical production was summarized by Miller as "the heart of the beast." Each writer revealed a different approach to his art — and they all valued the heterogeneity of their attitudes. There was a humorous awareness of their role as survivors and as active participants in a self-limiting profession. One could also feel in the course of the colloquy a growing sense of community among these diverse writers. These excerpts focus on Miller's contribution to the panel.*

As moderator, I began the discussion by quoting Shaw on the need for political theatre: "The great dramatist has something better to do than to amuse either himself or his audience. He has to interpret life…to pick out the significant incidents from the chaos of daily happenings and arrange them so that the relation to one another will become significant, thus changing us from bewildered spectators of a monstrous confusion to men intelligently conscious of the world and its destinies." Then I asked the panelists to what degree a playwright's work is shaped by world events and by the country he lives in.

Fugard said that it was impossible to tell a South African story that didn't have political resonance. For him, a play begins when the external specifics of a story run parallel to a very private need to make a personal statement. Shawn talked about facing a kind of blank wall, then finding a little door in that wall and "a bit of light glitters through, and I think how exciting that is, and so I'll write about that."

AM: Well, listening to you guys, I'm sitting here thinking, what really sets a play off is probably some overflow of love, even if it's the love of a form. If I suddenly see a way of telling a story, or if I find an ending, I can work backward. I find it very difficult to work from the beginning and go forward. I don't know why; it just is. Sometimes you come upon a language accent which sets off a kind of laughter, or joy. It's like the world is full of music but you can't follow the tune and then suddenly, in all that chaos, you can hear a tune go by that you can repeat. There's a lot of mimicry in it to me. The sound of it. If I can't hear it, then I don't write as well.

But to come back to the political side, I've seen the political element rise and fall several times. That is, in the 1930s, while I was still in college, a play couldn't be thought of as being important if it didn't refer in some way to the political logjam that existed then. Odets was the reigning important playwright, although by Broadway standards, he was delivering one failure after another. He was regarded as an important playwright but apparently not enough people wanted to see his plays. Then we got into the war and came out of that war and for a little moment in the 1940s, it was respectable to deal with political themes. I'm thinking of *State of the Union*, which was a comedy that dealt with elections. But soon if you said the word political in relation to a play it meant it was not artistic, it was propaganda.

Those were the years when Brecht could not be produced here, because everybody said, well, it's propaganda, which indeed it was. But it was something else too. After *The Price* opened, Walter Kerr said that I would drive the remaining audience out of the theatre completely, because my inspiration came from political convictions and that people wanted a spontaneous sort of authentic feeling — and entertainment. What he meant was, "Don't give me any metaphors." It had gone that far and people thought that Tennessee Williams was the perfection of the nonpolitical writer and therefore the most artistic writer. He might have felt insulted by that. I never discussed it with him as such, but I know he was very interested in politics.

Politics is the word for the distribution of power. You can't move without politics. It infiltrated the PEN meeting [in New York] yesterday. I had to remind them that there are bad governments, but I remember when the government helped a lot. I couldn't have gone through college without the government. I got $15 a month from the National Youth Adminstration. It paid my rent at the University of Michigan. Without that, I would have had to go out and do something else. When I got out of school, I was on the WPA [the federal Works Project Administration], like Saul Bellow, Orson Welles, Joseph Cotten. I could name a long list of people who were fed and given bed and board by the government for a while.

We've really turned against the humanist tradition to such a degree that now we're left with an anarchism which isn't even anarchism. It's just a blur, it's formless. It simply repeats its own concentration on the navel. So I agree, I think that the statement of Shaw's is terrific.

MG: If I heard you correctly, you were making a case for Tennessee Williams as a political writer.

AM: He wasn't a political writer, but look at *Cat on a Hot Tin Roof*: a distribution of property by a big landowner trying to give it to his offspring. The struggle in that play is around who is capable of carrying on this society. It may be the one that isn't the most charming, but somebody has to open the store in the morning. And if you've got a store, you have a problem. And without the power and politics, that play can't exist.

The only argument I can see in all this is that we have had a kind of prejudice in American culture which tells us that the world of power is somehow separated from the rest of mankind's pursuits, instead of being perhaps its most tragically *dangerous* expression. Is it really a complete accident that we've got an actor as the President right now? That's a marvelous imaginary idea. That's an act of the public imagination.

MG: Isn't it strange that politics has been moving more toward movies and television? I don't see playwrights today dealing with subjects such as nuclear annihilation.

AM: In the last ten years, movies and television have dealt far more often with matters of great import than the stage has. There have been numerous well-done movies and some television on what we used to call great issues. And in the theatre hardly at all. The theatre has become far more inward looking when formerly it was the extroverted art. I'm not sure I know the reasons. We've obviously delimited the New York audience to those people who can pay the price. As we all know, the schoolteacher isn't there, the ordinary civil service employee can't afford to go, students very rarely, etc. So we've got a skimming of the population. And maybe that has had some effect on what is appreciated, what they want from that art.

If we had a more democratic art, maybe it would be otherwise. I think of England, where probably they're dealing more with public issues, and more extroverted art. But it's also a theatre that is first of all cheaper by some good percentage. And it is, to some degree, subsidized so that the public has got a chance to see it. Maybe that's part of the reason. But I've found the theatre here has turned into an art form that is ingrown. It's super-sophisticated. Very often the theatre relies on cultural cues of a small group of people who get the signal rather than reinterpreting the material into a universal language.

FUGARD: That's a very provocative thought. Something like inbreeding, in a sense.

AM: That's a good word, yes. Too often, the theatre talks to itself. The black audience, the working people, the rest of them who wouldn't understand these clues, aren't there.

MG: Isn't it strange that politics has been moving more toward movies — a popular form — and you're making the case for theatre becoming an elitist art, even as that audience goes out to see *Cats*.

AM: They do go to see the musicals pre-eminently. We used to think that a hit ran a couple of seasons. I don't think a straight play now could look forward to that popularity.

AM: I just came from Lithuania a few weeks ago. A Soviet novelist named Aitmatov Chingiz wrote this terrific book, which was interpreted as an attack on Stalinism. And yet he's one of the biggest guys in the Communist Party and the Writers Union. I saw a play in Lithuania based on his novel. It's a powerful thing. I said, "How does that work?" One woman said, "Well, when he speaks he lies, but when he writes he tells the truth." And that's true of a lot of us. It's not that we're lying. It's that verbalizing something automatically eliminates a lot of the emotional connections which give them their truth. So what you're doing is giving a resumé of what you felt.

Mamet said that the question was about the will of the people versus the will of the individual: "We've all had the experience of getting whacked on the head one time, two times and saying, 'I don't care, I don't care. I'll go on and I will be heard.'"

AM: A lot of plays don't get written because the writer lacks a certain characterological toughness. You know, to be a playwright you not only have to be a writer, you have to be an alligator. A lot of writers are not alligators. I mean, in my lifetime I've known ten or twelve people who were really talented people, but they couldn't take the abuse. A playwright lives in an occupied country. He's the enemy. And if you can't live that way you don't stay.

MG: Why do you say alligator?

FUGARD: His skin.

AM: It's tough! He's got to be able to take a whack, and he's got to swallow bicycles and digest them. [*general laughter*] There is a repression, I think, finally as a result of the prevailing taste, which is re-enforced by critics who voice it. There has been a kind of an automatic admiration of the parodistic idea. In other words, it's better that the emotion not be directly expressed. The theatre has eliminated a lot of pain. I remember a time when it was directly the opposite, where the needle was north, namely, that important work was thought to be work that never let the audience off the hook.

All the plays that I was trying to write, all the plays that playwrights like O'Neill were trying to write, that Tennessee was writing, these were plays that would grab an audience by the throat and not release them, rather than presenting an emotion which you could observe and walk away from. I admire a play like *Amadeus* technically, but I saw Mozart's dying as a kind of a joke in that play. I know Peter Shaffer didn't intend it that way but the audience takes it as a real laugh riot. Every time Mozart laid his pen to paper, it was a masterpiece of some kind. When you think of the ones that he never got to write and idiocy of his dying at that age. The way it was presented, it made us feel remote.

In any case, whether it's better or worse, it would never have been done that way through the 1940s and into the 1950s. Which dares a little discussion because I think the real chasm came for us with Beckett. It's not just Beckett, it's the whole absurd department. Because that distanced pain a lot. Maybe life is too painful now. I know very responsible people who say, "I don't want to go to the theatre and experience pain. I don't want to be gripped. I want two hours to go by where I have quote-unquote pleasure." Aesthetically we are aware of the pain in Beckett, but I wonder if it's not too abstract for many people.

Shawn said it was terribly hard today for a writer to write truthfully about the suffering of an individual person, even though there were people suffering the tragedies that Willy Loman suffered. He added, "It would be absolutely my dream to be able to write a play about that suffering, and yet I'm unable to."

AM: I absolutely agree with you. I don't really think a Blanche DuBois or a Willy Loman would be forthcoming today. Certainly the critical fraternity would say, well, it's a little too *lush* emotionally.

MG: I would think that if there were an equivalent of Willy Loman today, it would be overwhelming.

AM: Two years ago, to pick an arbitrary time, I would have said you were wrong. I think that we may be in a moment of shift again. Maybe we've come to the end of what I call the abstraction of emotion. It is possible in the theatre as in music that a little change in emphasis changes everything. To get that catharsis, there has to be a very fine line between what this thing means and what it is emotionally. If you go in one direction, it just becomes pathetic, and in the other direction it becomes quite abstract and we don't get the man in the middle. In other words, somehow a work has to endanger the people. We've got to endanger their common equilibrium.

Since everything is OK in this society, they just let us talk. In a repressive society, the word is dynamite, it's simply dynamite.

FUGARD: Heiner Müller's remark yesterday at that PEN panel

was frightening. He said that in his country [East Germany] words could still kill. In America, they can't kill anyone.

AM: Our problem here is not political censorship. It's the commercial censorship. It's a commercial choice. If you're with it, you're OK. If you're not with it in some way, you're way outside there, just as outside as you could be in a repressive society.

MG: Müller also said that the primary problem with the American people was economics. The question was raised: if the economic troubles of the American theatre could be solved, would there be a political language that would be heard? In effect, he was asking if political playwrights and plays existed.

Mamet answered with a long discussion about the body politic ending with an analysis of Tolstoy's use of power in War and Peace. *Soon we were off on a vigorous discussion of the theatre critics at* The New York Times, *and whether or not they represented the readership — or the electorate — of the newspaper.*

MG: I think if you look at the range of people who have held the various critical positions at the *Times*, from Stark Young through Brooks Atkinson on to today, you'll see that they really are individuals.

AM: Incidentally, this is a political conversation. It is what I mean by politics.

MG: Arthur, you've said that the economics of the theatre is really one of the most boring subjects to speak about and yet in the end it is the most consequential in terms of the continuing validity of today's theatre.

AM: It is the heart of the beast.

MG: Is there any solution?

Fugard said that if ever he came up against a wall again in South Africa, he would do as he did with The Blood Knot. *He would "beg, borrow and steal the bucks," find a space and do the play. "Is that not possible for you chaps?"*

AM: It is. But all the levels are quite different. See, we have levels of expense Off Broadway now that are simply breathtaking. I don't know — where could you go?

FUGARD: Can I ask a question, because I don't know how this system works? You have written a new play, David, and it involves two actors. And we're sick and tired of this whole economic scene, but we're going to try and survive in New York. You come to Wally and to me and you say, "Come on, chaps, let's do it." And we say, "let's find an attic. Let's put up some lights and let's do it." Do you see anything to stop us?

Mamet said no, except for problems with Actors Equity and the fire marshall. If necessary, they could form a theatre club.

AM: Well, you could do it up to a point. Even if you're a club, and you've got, say, 75 people coming into somebody's living room regularly — they'll get there. Then we have another problem. You and Wally are in this play, and Mel Gussow comes to see it. He finds out about it. OK, and it's an event, right? Wally is simply fantastic — [*to Fugard*] you're all right, but Wally is absolutely fantastic.

FUGARD: [*laughs*] I don't like this story anymore now.

AM: And three movie guys come in and say to Wally, "We have a great film that you would be marvelous in."

And Wally says, "No, I don't want to leave this play." And they say, "Well, it's $30,000 a week." And after about a month, Wally's looking for his rent money and he says, "If I did it for just one week..."

And it begins to go like that. The Group Theatre was the archtypical example of this. They bucked the system for four, five, six years. But they were so damn good that every time they opened a show some Hollywood guy would say, "Franchot Tone, here's a movie." And then he looks around and says, "Jesus Christ, what am I eating cheese sandwiches for?" Then the theatre was vitiated. We're talking about an elitist idea, aren't we? We're not reaching into the great unwashed out there in Newark.

So my question is, why in the hell must we hide in a closet to do our work? You mean that we aren't allowed as artists to head a proper theatre? I go to visit actors Off Broadway, and they're all huddled in some toilet where all the clothes are hanging, and everybody says, "Isn't it wonderful?" What is so wonderful about this? I wouldn't put my dogs in there! The water is rusty in the sink, the women can't find any place to change. It's appalling! And uptown there are billionaires living in 46 rooms. I don't get the joke there. I think we deserve better than that. I don't mean we should all be treated like kings, but at least not like bums.

MG: Is there anything anyone wants to say in summary — or not in summary?

AM: Let's give three cheers for the theatre! Or three and a half. You know, our audience now has heard everything three times and we need to get people who haven't heard it yet. The Russians have a wonderful phrase, *the true word*, meaning the quote-unquote truth is what they want in the theatre, an expression of some kind of an insight that would tell them how to live, not how to amuse themselves.

November 18, 1986

"There's nobody up here but us chickens"

Early in 1987, two new one-act plays by Arthur Miller, I Can't Remember Anything *and* Clara, *were scheduled to open at Lincoln Center. Collectively they were titled* Danger: Memory! *This was the first time his work was at Lincoln Center since 1964, when* Incident at Vichy *was presented at the Vivian Beaumont Theatre. On November 18, 1986, we met for the first in a series of conversations. I picked him up at his Manhattan apartment and we walked to a neighborhood restaurant. It was noisy; we were flooded with sound, both spoken and musical. I began by remarking on his activity. In addition to the one-acts, there was a production of* All My Sons *coming up on public television and* The American Clock *was moving from the Cottesloe to the Olivier at London's National Theatre. His memoir,* Timebends, *was also scheduled to be published in 1987 on both sides of the Atlantic.*

AM: I've never been this busy. I don't know why it all piled up, but it certainly did. Europe has been terrific. There's a new production of *The Crucible* in Hungary of all places — again — apparently this time for political reasons. And Francois Perrier is doing *Salesman* in Paris. I also have *The Archbishop's Ceiling* in the RSC's Pit. There had been a production at the Bristol Old Vic about a year and a half ago, which I didn't see. Those who have seen this [RSC] production say the other was better.

MG: That's a first: being able to compare two productions of *The Archbishop's Ceiling*.

AM: The RSC production is sold out, and they'll go on with it indefinitely. And Alan Ayckbourn is directing *A View from the Bridge* in February [at the National Theatre in

London]. There's an actor there [Michael Gambon] who they're talking about as the new Olivier. The National, which usually has trouble with money, called me and said this was going to be a great event, and would I come. I said, "Well you're going to have to pay for it." So I may go over there.

MG: How do you explain the renewed interest in your work?

AM: It may be that the social and moral concerns in those plays are now on the agenda again. For a long time, there was an affectation to the effect that no judgments could be made about anything. Of course, these plays, implicitly or explicitly, create a moral universe. And maybe that's new.

MG: One charge was that many of your plays are of their period, that a play like *All My Sons* dealt with a specific issue at a specific time. The feeling was that *The Crucible* dealt with a particular issue at two different times, and that *The American Clock* was a Depression play.

AM: With *All My Sons,* it's not just this little guy causing a couple of airplanes to fall down. Now it's the space shuttle, and it turns out that nobody is taking responsibility.

MG: Do you think the morality of the plays is the major factor in the increased interest?

AM: I don't know what the major factor is. I think it's a new factor. In the last decade, the movies took up issues such as *All My Sons* does. I'm thinking of that one that Jane Fonda did [*The China Syndrome*] and the one that [Mike] Nichols directed [*Silkwood*]. That's dropped out of theatre. Maybe that's part of the rediscovery. In England there is a steady supply of plays at the RSC and the National as well as in the regional theatres, plays about what you could call social issues, like this one about [Rupert] Murdoch [*Pravda* by Howard Brenton and David Hare]. That play could have been written by the WPA theatre, although I don't know if they could have done it as well.

MG: You might say that in England, political theatre comes

with the territory. David Mamet has said that if you're an English playwright that's what you write about.

AM: The audience here hasn't felt pain in a long time. There's no great systemic upheaval.

MG: The other day I went to see a revival of *The Skin of Our Teeth* Off Broadway and it seemed dated where *All My Sons,* which seemed to be of its period, is not. Sometimes I think that perhaps it's the specificity of a work that makes it survive.

AM: The attitude in *Skin of Our Teeth* is basically sentimental: Wilder's positive feelings towards humanity are enough to float this ship which manifestly is sinking without a trace — namely civilization. For no good reason, he's saying, don't worry, we'll survive. That was also true of Saroyan: an implicit sentimental optimism. There's nothing like that in *All My Sons.*

MG: Will we survive?

AM: It's a damn good question. I always used to say, somebody is going to light a match in a warm room and blow the whole fucking thing up. That Chernobyl thing is the lighting of the match. Literally, it's like going down a hill in a truck. Shut off the engine and remove the brakes and see what happens. You know I worked in the Brooklyn Navy Yard during the war. They used to have these unbelievable cranes picking up tonnage. They were on rails and they would go around the yard like monsters, moving big steel plates from one point to another. There was some guy running the crane, about four stories up, looking down at these little mice running around. One day he got out of the crane and left it. Here's a crane moving by itself at a pretty good speed. Someone had to catch up with it, climb up to it. What kind of man would do this? That's the kind of thing that gives you pause. There's no time to react.

My daughter, who is 24 now, is of a generation that melodramatizes itself a bit. The convention among those kids is that the world is not going to let them mature to old age. You send those kids to see *The Skin of Our Teeth*? *All My Sons* is much more modern than that. Stoppard has this attitude that everything is happening on the edge of a cliff, and the actors are about to be pushed off. [*laughs*] That amuses me. I feel that's very contemporary. In my work, the same thing takes a different form. Somebody is going to die in this play, or somebody has died, as in *After the Fall*. Wilder is writing after the victory; I'm writing before the defeat.

MG: With you, the victory never comes?

AM: The assumption of Wilder is that we have made it. I was driving in to New York this morning and the guy on the radio said, "We're going to have to close midtown Manhattan within the next few years. You can't get the cars in." I was laughing with Inge. It took me an hour and 40 minutes to get from Connecticut, which is 100 miles away, to the West Side Highway; it took three quarters of an hour to get from 60th Street on the West Side Highway to Eighth Avenue and 58th Street. All that horsepower — it's not going anywhere. Nobody's going anywhere.

MG: Do you feel closer to Samuel Beckett than to Thornton Wilder?

AM: Absolutely. You see what hope there is in my plays is left in the lap of the audience. It's a challenge whether you want to hope or not — because the evidence is pretty bad. You've got one man who stands up there and says, "It's all bullshit."

MG: Why should the audience hope?

AM: Because they want to. They want to hope that, through him, this will spread, that there can be resistance to falsehood.

MG: Does that mean that theatregoers come out of *Waiting for Godot* and they think somehow, somewhere, someone will come?

AM: That's right.

MG: Maybe tomorrow.

AM: Or in an hour. I didn't see him on this block, but he may be around the corner.

MG: Cynicism is part of your survival?

AM: It's not cynicism. I'm always ready to believe. If you read the Book of Job and you add up the evidence, the case is hopeless. Job should put a bullet in his head. But the sun is going to come up tomorrow and he might feel differently. [*laughs*] That's about as good as you can put it. Look at the evidence. He's absolutely *crushed* by reality.

MG: As you say that, I'm thinking of all the people who die in your plays.

AM: Very bad evidence. Not a good sign. One of the ones who noticed this was the chairman of the House UnAmerican Activities Committee, Mr. [Congressman Francis E.] Walter, who said to me, "With all your talent, why do you write so tragically about this country?" He wanted the good news. I can only bring the good news after the bad news. The good news is simply that we're here and we've got an obligation to ourselves.

Incidentally, that's the question Russian writers used to be asked. Why write tragedy? We want romance, romantic optimism. I think now it's a different case. When I talked to Gorbachev, he said, "All I ask of literature is that the fate of humanity is involved; the rest is up to you." That it be not trivial. That to me is a given; it comes with the territory. Why in the face of that we should have anything other than complete nihilism, that's the question. And I go back to biology. If you look at the child before he is educated, he wants to live. That's reality.

MG: As you get older, does your attitude about writing change?

AM: I enjoy it more now, because I think I have less of a dependency on what anybody else makes of my work. One reason for that is practical. For example, *The American Clock* ran here for about four days, maybe a week, and I go to London eight or ten years later and see it and audiences are standing up and cheering. And *The Archbishop's Ceiling*, we couldn't even bring in to New York. That was my fault because I made changes in it that I should never have made. I went back to the original for this production. I guess I simply have a longer view. The critics are much younger than I am. The idea of one's peers is a little weakened. I love good reviews better than anything. The shock to the ego when you get bad reviews!

MG: You've lost your critical peers and also your playwriting peers.

AM: There's nobody up here but us chickens. [*laughs*]

MG: Who are your peers?

AM: In this country, I don't know of anybody even close to my age in the theatre as a writer.

MG: At one point, when you, Tennessee Williams and William Inge were all on Broadway, didn't you feel you were in a much more active theatrical environment?

AM: It's difficult to define, but there was what I would call a theatre culture. A theatre culture means a lot of plays going on, most of them trivial, a few of them reflecting the moment. They may not be masterpieces, but they are reflecting the hour in which one is living. Actors trying to be contemporary people. An audience that has been to more than two plays in the last five years, and knows that this play is different from that play and related to that other play. That may exist, unbeknownst to me, but I don't sense it. OK, I'm hoping that we can create some kind of viable audience at Lincoln Center that is passionately interested in this, but I don't know if that's possible anymore.

I saw [John] Guare's play [a revival of *The House of Blue Leaves* at Lincoln Center] and I was really happily surprised that so many young people were in the audience, under 28 or 26. I went to see Spalding Gray. That was a young audience, although you would have thought that would have attracted an older audience. I enjoyed that immensely.

MG: When you and Tennessee were running neck and neck, did you feel a sense of competitiveness?

AM: I don't want to sound insanely generous, but I used to hope that he would have a big hit, partially for selfish reasons. I was already hearing people say, ah, there's nothing new in the theatre. I would desperately try to think of things for them to go to see. My sense of doom was very sharp. And this is back in the 1950s. They mustn't get disillusioned with this theatre. And the more the merrier. That doesn't mean that I wouldn't want better reviews than he got. But I certainly wanted him to get a terrific reception. He wrote a letter that I got a copy of just two days ago, which is to this point. There's a man writing his biography. We met quite by chance and he said, "Oh, you're mentioned in a couple of his letters." So he sent me these letters and in the letter which he sent to Audrey Wood from Rome, he says, everybody sends me these notices of *Death of a Salesman*. The gist of it was that he was nervous and happy. He read the play and he loved it.

He liked me too and I liked him. There was that side of him, plus the competitive side. But I'm sure it excited him to know that he was not alone. I wish we had 25 other playwrights, for my own selfish reasons. And I suppose what I'm doing now is totally unrealistic, but I still get excited about it. I know that I planted that seed that's going to be going on forever. It'll pop up in India, Hungary. Nobody promised me a rose garden.

In fact, years ago when I was on the Dramatists Guild board, I made a few regrettable remarks to the effect that maybe we were taking too much money out of the theatre and what we had to do was start a movement to reduce everybody's take. That caused a meeting to be held. Mr. Shubert came, they got the unions in and I made a speech to them. The ticket price then was probably $10 or $8. I said, "You know a lot of my friends don't come anymore because they haven't got the money for it. I think we ought to find a way to reduce our costs." Lee Shubert just sat there. Herman Shumlin got up, screaming that producers are starving to death. I turned to Mr. Shubert and said, "What do you think?" He never answered.

MG: Tennessee always had this thing about wanting one more major Broadway success.

AM: Yes, I would, too. Not Broadway. I couldn't care less where it was. I could see it at the Vivian Beaumont and play it for twelve weeks. The great thing about the theatre, from my experience, is that it does go on, continually.

MG: But you do want, as you say, more respect.

AM: You know, everybody's forgotten but Ibsen ran for three weeks in Norway. Then he went to Germany where the plays ran a little longer. He made his living from his books, selling those plays. I would like to simplify the whole image a little more for myself. Say I get eight weeks, with a terrific production. It's worth writing plays. I have to say that, because the other way is hopeless: the dependency upon producers, critics, audiences. We are close to the bottom.

MG: Have you always been able to make a living in the theatre?

AM: I shouldn't say I made it all out of the theatre because I made some out of films, but no great fortune. Basically my income has come from productions here and abroad, which are not necessarily Broadway productions. You make a lot on Broadway but I would bet that I made more from amateur rights and regional theatre productions.

MG: More from *Salesman* than anything else?

AM: No. *Salesman* is not produced nearly as much as *The Crucible*. The reason for that is obvious. For *Salesman*, you need a big actor. A lot of companies don't have that. And secondly there are a lot of parts for women in *The Crucible*. Most of these companies have a lot of women. And it's a much easier play to make happen.

MG: You write because you want to write but also because you have to sustain an income.

AM: You know, I enjoy doing other things: making furniture —

and I have children all over the place. Big ones, little ones, grandchildren. I have three grandchildren in California. So I could occupy myself easily enough. But there's an intensification of feeling when you create a play, which doesn't exist in me in any other thing I can do. It's a way of spiritually living. I guess people who take drugs know the difference between being sober and being on something. Once it's started, there's a pleasure there that's indescribable. It doesn't exist in real life, because you're really making the whole thing happen.

MG: While you're doing it?

AM: While you're doing it. You get swept up in a free emotional life, being all those other people.

MG: What happens when you're stymied?

AM: Then it's agony. I wrote a play, which would be a four-act play, and I've got three of them. I broke off about 1984. Spent about two years on it. I'm hoping that when I pick it up again, it will all be clear. I don't know whether it will. You start off, you think you're going on a voyage, and the boat gets to the middle of the ocean and runs out of gas.

MG: You only need one more act.

AM: That's the agony,

MG: What is that play about?

AM: It's about marriages. I guess it's about life being an ironical trap, which requires laughter. But there are many refractions of this work, of society, of sexual relations. It's hard to describe it.

MG: Is this your first comedy since *The Creation of the World*?

AM: Well, it's no more comic than some of the others I've written, but I'm laughing. But I used to laugh when I wrote *Death of a Salesman*.

I'm not sure it's going to be a comedy. I'm looking at it from the lip of the grave.

MG: Sounds like Beckett.

AM: That's right. I've never met him. Have you?

MG: Yes. He can be quite approachable — but he hates to talk about his work.

AM: I don't like it either. You know what you find yourself doing: You've got to capsulize. Otherwise you talk about a two-hour play for at least two hours.

MG: Tennessee could talk openly about the most personal sexual matter, but when it came to his creativity, he would close down. His explanation was: that was too personal.

AM: To objectify the whole thing: there's a friend of mine who is a biophysicist who works over at Rockefeller. I always had a passing interest in science. I went up to visit his lab. He has computers there that can move things in all directions 360 degrees. I asked him how this is possible. He gave me some figures, which I can't remember, of the number of inputs into that machine to fill up that space to make this happen. If you start to write, it's coming out from when you're three years old, when you had lunch yesterday, out of something somebody told you twelve years ago, out of some hope you had that arose from one word somebody said. The number of impulses are infinite.

MG: But don't you know the things that motivate you to sit down and begin to write something?

AM: If I hear the way somebody speaks, above all if I feel affection for that, if I like it, I can start improvising on him or her. Maybe I have the vaguest idea that somebody's going to live or die or whatever. Without that, I can't begin. It's a bit like music, I suppose, but musicians are more abstract than that. I write with my ears more than with my brains. I never write until I can hear it.

MG: The general misconception about your writing process is that you sit down with a structure: this play is going to say thus and so.

AM: That's the last thing I would do. It's a mistake because the structures are strong so you feel they must have been there from the beginning. For example, these two one-acts [*I*

Can't Remember Anything and *Clara*] and *The American Clock*. I know the feeling that it should give, that's all. And *The American Clock* is a special case because it's an episodic play. With *I Can't Remember Anything*, I had no idea where it was going.

MG: Where did that play start?

AM: It comes from sound, those people going on at each other.

MG: You heard two old people talking in a restaurant?

AM: No, I know them better than that. I hear them. I start laughing. I know I can move in and start to shape. The same with Willy Loman. In the case of *The Crucible,* I can't have heard any of it. What really set me off was reading dialogue from the trial. I went up to Salem to research the record, I wasn't sure I would even write the play. Incidentally I have a feeling the Elizabethans must have worked that way. You hear it better in the minor writers. *Fair Maid of the West* was on at Stratford when I was there. This is the way they talk. With the British actors, it's more in their blood, than in ours. The way they did it was with the gusto of real speech.

MG: For you, language is most important.

AM: Absolutely. It amuses me when a critic says I don't have any sense of language. Could anyone read *A View from the Bridge* or *The Crucible,* and believe the same writer wrote both of them?

MG: Which is your voice?

AM: I'm a mime in those plays. My voice is probably more cultivated or educated, although when I speak in public I sound like Brooklyn.

MG: With Tennessee Williams, his voice was clear through every play.

AM: Because he was really close to home always.

MG: What's the difference with you?

AM: I haven't been that close to home always. *All My Sons* is taking place in Ohio. If anybody will listen carefully, it's lower middle-class Ohio speech. *Salesman* is Brooklyn. But of a certain specific level of Brooklyn. Biff says, "I've been remiss." How can anybody in Brooklyn say "remiss?" Of course it's a sign of a certain elevation on his part.

MG: Which of your plays is closest to home?

AM: I would say *Salesman*. It represented my youth as a writer. Memories. I left home when I was eighteen or nineteen. I lived in the Midwest. My home ceased to interest me.

MG: Do you think of your life and work in periods?

AM: I suppose I'm more interested in the irony of existence. In *Clara*, the second of these two plays, the death is there, but it's there before the play begins. It's an adjustment to death, it's a way of carrying death.

MG: As you get older, do you think of death being closer?

AM: I think it becomes slightly less awesome. When you're 29 or 30 or earlier, the idea is impossible. But I've had so many friends die. I know I can't do things now that I could do before. I was just out in the yard two days ago running a machine, which I had to walk behind. I never thought twice about it before. I had to pull it up a hill and I had to stand there and catch my breath and I thought, I would never have thought about this. I would have done it and then done something else. Now I have to stop and think, well, that's that one. I feel good because I was able to do it at that moment. I guess it's some stupid kind of optimism, which overcomes what's left of the brain. There's no other adjustment to it that I can accept. You can get blue and discouraged.

MG: Would you ever get so depressed that you would think about killing yourself?

AM: I guess I don't think that I have the right to feel I'm that important, that I would take the world on my shoulders quite that way. I want to be able to do something about it.

MG: What if, like Hemingway, you were unable to write anymore?

AM: I think he was ill, physically ill. He did a lot of drinking, and brain cells are destroyed by alcohol.

MG: Do you have any bad habits?

AM: [*pause*] Yes, I waste a lot of time. The worst is, I enjoy wasting it.

MG: What do you call wasting time?

AM: Reading newspapers. When I think of the pile of *New York Times* I have read, that would send me out of this world in a spirit of great disgruntlement. That's a bad habit. Every day I go through the goddamn paper. My wife says, "Well, what is in it?" I look up and say, "I don't know." Think of it: I could have learned Persian or Greek. I could have read Homer three or four times. I could have at least learned Yiddish.

MG: But from reading the newspapers, you find out what's going on today.

AM: What they *tell* you is going on. What they *think* is going on. I often wonder, is that the novel of our time? The *Times* has these long pieces. There are continuous stories. Someone is indicted. He has got to have a trial. It goes on and on. It's a continuous thread.

MG: Can you go cold turkey for a period of time and not read anything?

AM: I've got to know what's going on.

MG: Is conversation a time waster?

AM: No, I don't think so. I never had a wasted conversation. I always get something out of that. I fool around on my place. I repair machinery that I should send out to somebody to do. I stare out the window a lot more than I should, and create business for myself. That gets me to a different subject and this is a category of a dream. If I had a theatre that I was connected to, a theatre of my peers, a working theatre, with a good group of actors, I probably would have written a number of more plays. I had one experience like that in my life and that was before Lincoln Center collapsed. I had done *After the Fall,* and Harold Clurman came to me and said, "Look, we've got to have another play. Do you have anything else?" And I wrote *Incident at Vichy.* And it worked out magically; there was a part for every actor in the company. That never occurred to me. There was an excitement about it. You didn't have to run around finding producers. If there had been some relationship, roughly of that kind...In England, there's an approximation of that. They have ten, twelve playwrights floating around, these two great theatres [the National and the RSC]. It's very important. It's a defense against the outside. "We're all in this together."

MG: Instead of writing more plays, what did you do?

AM: It all collapsed. I didn't write. I was terribly discouraged, partly because of the collapse of that theatre, partly because I sensed before the theatre opened that there was a hostility, a negative cynicism, maybe because [Robert] Whitehead was a Broadway producer.

MG: I always thought that Harold Clurman should have been head of the theatre instead of only being its dramaturg.

AM: First of all, they wouldn't have given it to him. If they had given it to him, he might have risen to it, but he had a tendency to move away from any real responsibility.

MG: If Clurman had either been head of that theatre or been named the chief drama critic of *The New York Times,* he might have changed the theatre. In the case of Lincoln Center, the board wanted instant success.

AM: With Kazan and Clurman and Whitehead, the idea was to have a pure repertory theatre — which I'm not for, by the way. We should choose actors on an impromptu basis. For a repertory company, you have to have five Oliviers and a couple of Richardsons.

December 12, 1986

"Some good parts for actors"

Arthur Miller and his wife Inge Morath live in Roxbury, Connecticut, in a rural area populated by many people in the arts. I had been visiting Martha Clarke, the director and choreographer, who lives nearby in Sherman, Connecticut. She is a friend of mine and also of the Millers. On a brisk winter morning, the Millers met me at a dance studio where Martha was in rehearsal with a new theatre piece. I followed the Millers back to their home, a large, sprawling house on top of a knoll. Several years ago, there was a fire on the property and parts of the house had to be rebuilt. In the house are sculptures by Alexander Calder (and a Calder portrait of Miller) and drawings by Saul Steinberg, both friends of the Millers; Morath's photographs, and various tables and cabinets built by Miller, who prides himself on the craftmanship of his carpentry. There was a chill in the air and Miller made a fire in the fireplace.

At this point, Sid Caesar was scheduled to star with Geraldine Fitzgerald in one of the one-acts, I Can't Remember Anything *(subsequently he withdrew from the cast and was replaced by Mason Adams). Miller is a great fan of Caesar — and of Caesar's comedy — and our conversation began with him.*

AM: I'll tell you how I met him. I did an article for *Esquire* three years ago. They asked me to write about the McCarthy period as I experienced it. I went to the Museum of Broadcasting to look at tapes of the Army-McCarthy hearings, which I remembered vaguely, but I had forgotten the series of events. I sat there watching. The door opens and in walks Sid Caesar, whom I had never met. He had written a book and was giving a lecture in an auditorium a few yards from the room in which I was sitting. He was going to talk to a whole roomful of young comedians. I said, "Are there that many young comedians?" He said, "The number's enormous and they're very good. I'm not ready yet. Do you mind if I sit down and wait?" He asked what I was doing, and I explained. It's interesting; he had been on *Your Show of Shows* [Caesar's popular weekly television series] during this period, and he didn't recognize McCarthy. I said to myself, he was probably just too busy, which was a wonderful comment on Caesar's life. So there was McCarthy, and Caesar watched him as if for the first time. On this black and white tape, McCarthy was in the process of showing a map of China. He blacked it out and over this vast geographical area it said "Communist" — and he combined it with the Soviet Union. Without a break, McCarthy said, "Edgar [sic] R. Murrow is a member of the American Civil Liberties Union," and paused. Caesar said [about McCarthy's blacking out of the map], "Oh, I get it. You just start painting and you paint the walls and the furniture and books and the ceiling and the floor and everybody sitting in the chairs." It was wonderful. [*laughs*]

MG: At the time, probably more people in America were watching Sid Caesar's show than the McCarthy hearings.

AM: He obviously hadn't been watching them. He was absolutely candid and funny as hell. He told me a couple of stories about himself. I never dreamed I would have him in a play. Anyway, I hadn't written these plays then. So when Greg [the director Gregory Mosher] called me up to tell me that Sid Caesar was going to be in my play, my heart stopped, and I thought, is he really going to be able to do this? Then I thought of the way he sat there talking to me. He seemed to be a very deep man, like someone who suffered a lot.

MG: How does it feel to be back at Lincoln Center?

AM: Well, I love it there. First of all, they've got 16,000 seats to sell [for the run of the play] and they've got 23,000 applications for the seats. That means we don't have to be in desperate anxiety about the critics. We're only there for eight weeks and that's just fine. The plays get launched. We've got a superb cast: Ken McMillan, James Tolkan and Geraldine Fitzgerald — and Sid Caesar. If we had a production on Broadway and we said we're going to run as long as we can run, I question whether I would be able to collect those actors.

MG: When you opened Lincoln Center with *After the Fall,* so much more was at stake. There was such anticipation.

AM: To put it in a nutshell, I talked to Olivier about it two years after that. The National Theatre was not yet in its new building. It was in those barracks and at the Old Vic [with temporary office accommodations near Waterloo Station]. When I saw him, he said, "What the hell is the matter with these people in New York? We were seven years at Chichester before we opened, and I would say that at least 25 percent of the time we were blasted out of the water, but nobody thought we would have to close down." Of course, the principle behind the National Theatre was never adopted in New York. There was no budget here to pay the actors. We had eleven or twelve of them. You couldn't hang your firm's name on the back of an actor the way you could put one on the back of a seat or on a wall of the theatre. No one was about to subsidize an acting company. That's the heart of it.

MG: In England, it's not unusual to have a repertory company.

AM: Here it had to be invented. I remember [Robert] White-head trying to tell that board, especially [the chairman] George Woods, that the more successful this kind of theatre became, the more money it was going to lose. To Woods, this was simply mathematically impossible. If we do four productions, you've got four sets to store, all those costumes to store. You've got to have people keeping those costumes up, people working on wigs. You've got a staff. In a Broadway theatre, you're doing the one thing, and when you stop doing it, you close. *After the Fall* played to something like 92 percent capacity. *Incident at Vichy*, likewise. There was no dearth of customers. There was simply no economic way to pay for it any more than you could do with the symphony orchestra or the opera. You sell every seat in the opera and you still can't pay for it.

There is a reason why Lincoln Center theatre floundered: because George Woods never believed in it in the first place. And he was the head of it. Why didn't he believe in it? Well, there may have been good reasons. Maybe such a thing is not possible in this country. Whatever they are, Woods shouldn't have remained head of a "repertory company." But he did, and at the right time he drove a spike in its heart. Economically there was absolutely no reason to stop it, because the thing was making its way. The money made on tickets was as much as you could expect. Could you imagine building these buildings, setting up this company and designing it so that the first production would be Rex Harrison in a British commercial production of *Caesar and Cleopatra*. What I missed was the indignation from anywhere. The young people of the then avant-garde sneered at the whole thing. You think they would say, "Look this is our building." I made a few speeches, I said, "This is your building, why are you sitting there sneering at all this?"

MG: The few public attempts at repertory in America have been failures, for example the Brooklyn Academy of Music company. Perhaps the repertory idea in America is doubtful.

AM: If you look back at where it started, you realize it's more than doubtful. I suppose the whole idea must have started in the 17th or 18th century in Europe where some lord or baron or duke had his little court and had some players. First of all, there was a limited number of players. And they would say, let's do Plautus this week and we'll do a play by Jack Jones the next week. So you had the same group of people, of necessity. There was an integral reason in that society for that kind of organization. Of course we don't have anything like that. Why impose it upon us? What's the virtue? There's also a feeling that theatre should be a moneymaking operation, that it's a very lucrative business.

＊

MG: I wonder if we could discuss the arc of your work after *After the Fall*.

AM: Well I did *The Price* and *The Archbishop's Ceiling*, which is now at the Royal Shakespeare Company, and *The American Clock* and *The Creation of the World*, and I did two other one-acts which we did at Long Wharf [*Elegy for a Lady* and *Some Kind of Love Story*]. And these one-acts. And I've been working on a long, big play [*The Ride Down Mt. Morgan*], which took a lot of time, and I took time out to do this book [his autobiography, *Timebends*] and to write these two plays. Those plays are all quite different. I'm trying to find one principle behind them. [*thinks*] They're probably plays that are less subjective than the early ones, including *The Crucible*. But after *Salesman*, I went in the direction of a more objectified theatre. *The Crucible* was in part a reaction against some of the weeping surrounding *Salesman*. I wanted a more acerbic kind of a play. I wanted to create as much knowing as feeling.

MG: What do you mean by "the weeping surrounding *Salesman?*"

AM: I had a reaction against too much empathy surrounding the play. I wasn't prepared for wiping people out the way that play did. It seemed to me there was more being said there than simply a sad tale.

MG: You mean there was more emotion in it than you felt?

AM: I felt emotion, but I didn't think it was going to come pouring out that way.

87

MG: Why should that bother you?

AM: It did bother me in a way because I felt they weren't seeing Willy, they were just feeling him. And they weren't seeing the ironies, they were just feeling some tremendous welling up of pity. I suppose I reacted against that, and I wanted in *The Crucible* not to create somebody that they would just weep over, but that would arouse anger and awareness of what the terms were of these kinds of persecutions.

Incidentally, this may have nothing to do with it, but a week ago I was at my publisher, Aaron Asher, and in walked a lady, Yuen Cheng, who had spent six years in solitary confinement in Red China. She came out and wrote a fantastic book, which is called *Life and Death in Shanghai.* We both knew some of the same people in China. This woman was a very elegant lady who had been the wife of the Standard Oil Company's chief in China. They tortured her. That would have killed me. I don't know how she lived through it. Her book is a marvelous piece of literary work. I couldn't put it down.

She didn't expect to meet me there, and I didn't expect to meet her. I was just delivering 700 pages of my book to Aaron. And she was doing a little publicity for her book, which they are also publishing. She said, "Oh, I meet you at last." She said, "When I got out in 1979" — I think she said it was 1979 — "I was in Shanghai, and they had a production of *The Crucible,* and I saw that. I had been in prison since 1969. So the outside world had no meaning to me at all. I looked at that play and thought, how could he have known the Chinese situation?"

Now, you see: I'm glad of that because it means the play strikes the central nervous system of this kind of a social situation, no matter where it happens. And of course the Russians will say the same thing about this under Stalin. And that's what I wanted from that play. I didn't want them falling down in the aisle, weeping over John Proctor. I wanted them to see that nervous system, because *that's* the emotion of the play, that's the *awesome* fact of it, that human beings can do this thing.

MG: Can't you have both?

AM: You can! Well, they're weeping for John Proctor, but they're also seeing him. That's the ideal thing, what I've always tried to do, make them see and feel at the same time. I just felt that *Salesman* went overboard a little bit too much. Now I've seen productions which have attempted to right that balance. I'm not sure they have succeeded.

MG: Critics might think that since *Salesman*, there has been a certain intellectual coldness about your work. Why doesn't he write plays with the emotional power of *Salesman*?

AM: That could be a failing, but it wasn't what I wanted to do. I did not want to overemotionalize this. It's not that I disown *Salesman*. I'm proud of it. But there were other things I wanted.

MG: The charge that I raised of intellectual coldness would be less against *The Crucible* than against *After the Fall,* and some of the other later work. How conscious was that on your part?

AM: Well, you see, in *After the Fall,* for example, I was really trying to do something, which I didn't know how to do on purely subjective levels. The play is about the kind of a person that is not Willy Loman. He's somebody who is always trying to figure out what happened to him. Willy is doing that in a way, but he'd rather not know. He would rather just succeed. On any terms. It's the difference between a more intellectualized human being and a less intellectualized one. And it would be false to him to pretend that he doesn't know what he wants. I wanted to write plays in which people on stage knew as much as the people in the audience — if that were possible.

I've seen a production of *After the Fall* in Italy. Zeffirelli did it. And Visconti did in Paris. The Italian one with

Monica Vitti was interesting. This was no great departure for them, apparently, from plays by Pirandello, from plays by numerous other European writers, where people were able to verbalize what they were feeling. Or even the French theatre of Giraudoux, where people could talk about what they were feeling. So Zeffirelli put Monica Vitti on stage with Giorgio Albertazzi who created an ambience of such intense search that I looked at it and I thought, the emotion is all there. It's just that when we — Americans, and the British — begin to try to think on stage, we get very remote. When the Italian does it, he never for a moment separates this from the fever of thinking.

Inge and I watched Fellini's picture, *La Dolce Vita*, the other night. I have to tell you that we stopped in the middle. It was so boring. And I love Fellini. I love everything he does, and there are images in it that I will never forget. The opening scene with the big statue being carried by a helicopter across Rome. But the movie was spitballed together, in my opinion. I don't think he had a script. There were the same characters running through it: totally undramatic. I never remembered it being that long in the first place. And we couldn't keep our eyes open. It seemed to be going nowhere. And she was simply awful, that big blonde actress [Anita Ekberg]. You know what occurred to me, by the way. I think Fellini was taking off on Marilyn with that character. But Marilyn had a certain absolutely devastating charm. This one only had blonde hair.

You see this was an attempt by him to create an idea in images, and the idea was *La Dolce Vita*, this over-rich society where people are finally totally dispirited. They have no moral direction. Of course, it's laughable in one respect. What they thought of as being over-rich [*laughs*] when they made the movie — it's about on the level of the working class of New Milford [an affluent community next to Roxbury, where Miller lives]. It's hardly there! I had to interpolate it. Oh I see what he's getting at. He thinks that if a person has a Cadillac convertible...of course in Italy that size car would be an absurdity anyway. The symbolism had lost its punch because it was so grounded in the society.

MG: In its time, we thought it was the ultimate in decadence.

AM: You ought to see it now. It's not up to the middle-class level today, even in Italy. The lower middle class is far beyond that kind of thing, as far as my observation goes. Anyway, that was an attempt to intellectualize emotion, and I don't think it was happening in the film — now. I was not aware of the picture in relation to my play at that time.

MG: It was about the same period.

AM: It was. They were going to do *After the Fall* with Mastroianni in Rome. He came to see me at the Chelsea Hotel, and he said a marvelous line. I said, "What do you think of this situation?" He said, "You mean in the play?" I said, "Yes, what do you think of this woman?" He said, "Me personally?" I said, "Yes, what would you do?" He said, "Oh, I would take a walk." [*laughs*] At that time he was very eager to do the play, but he said he could only do it for some months because Fellini had a picture for him. I said, "What picture?" He said, "I don't know, he just said there was a picture." I said, "You don't know what the script is?" He said, "You never know what the script is. I come to the studio and he says, all right, you go over there and you play this kind of a scene." And that was 8½.

MG: To get back to emotion versus intellect: through your choice of protagonist in *After the Fall,* you locked yourself into that conflict by having Quentin a lawyer rather an artist himself. You're in an intellectualized framework rather than one that calls for an outpouring of emotion.

AM: To me, that is very exciting. I don't know why we can't admit that into the aesthetic realm. I don't see the conflict really. It's just a different kind of feeling. It's on a different level, but if you recall these two one-act plays, they're not unconscious people in those plays. In *I Can't Remember Anything*, the Sid Caesar character is an educated, feeling person. And she is too. She says her mother was head of the Boston College for Women. She's a cultured, cultivated woman. But the feeling is tremendous. Why not? Now, the second play, where the man's child is murdered, is trying to reach toward some center, a spiritual center so to speak, an irony which requires something more than the kind of dialogue that there is in *Death of a Salesman*. I think what we did in the theatre was to separate the subjective from the objective. I think it's a question of perspective too. *After the Fall* is being done more now. I think it meets a certain kind of feeling people have now, a feeling that they've got to look at their lives.

MG: Do you have any second or third thoughts about *After the Fall,* things you might have done differently?

AM: I never can think of doing anything differently. It's like your face. You can't think of changing your face.

MG: Tennessee was always rewriting his plays.

AM: I can't imagine doing that. They belong to a moment, a time and a development of your spirit. It's just inconceivable to me to try and go back over a play. Tennessee wasn't rewriting his longer plays, was he?

MG: He kept changing *Cat on a Hot Tin Roof,* and he wrote *Summer and Smoke* at least twice. He didn't rewrite *Streetcar.*

MG: To many people, *After the Fall* would be considered a problematic play, if not a failure. Admitting all the departure from the truth of Marilyn Monroe, the play dealt with something extraordinarily personal to you. I thought perhaps you might want to treat those elements again, and in your memoir [*Timebends*] you talk about some of them — about Marilyn — perhaps with a different approach and a greater degree of honesty.

AM: I talk about her in the book. I talk about that play too, and the way it started. The seed for that play came years earlier when we were married. Walter Wanger [the film producer] came to me to write a screenplay about Camus's *The Fall*. I didn't do it. I didn't feel like writing a screenplay. But the moral dilemma in Camus's book interested me. A man, a so-called self-described judge penitent who is now ceasing to lay moral judgment on the world, witnessed a woman committing suicide and failed to stop her. My question was: supposing he succeeded in stopping her? *After the Fall* was primarily to me almost totally a work in which I was trying to discover by what means, by what cathexis, anybody could seize the reality of his life, which can only be the question of how responsible he is for his life. That's what that play is about, and it's utilizing this experience for that end.

MG: Isn't it also about how responsible a man is for someone else's life?

AM: Yes. How can you separate them? It's impossible to separate them.

MG: The title is "after" Camus's *Fall*, as well?

AM: His fall too. What happens after, supposing he had done this, and after the fall from...innocence — that is the innocence of one's own responsibility? Once that innocence is finished, on what basis do you create the illusion of life? That's what that play's about.

MG: Would it have been a different play if Quentin had been a writer rather than a judge penitent?

AM: I don't know. How could it have been? You see, there's been a lawyer in every play I've ever written, and I never knew that until some PhD wrote about it. The law is, of course, a metaphor for the moral order of man. The lawyer in my plays always brings in the question of the continuity of the world. It's one thing for you to make an excuse for yourself, but if that were applied broadly to the world, could it go on? That's what the lawyer's doing.

MG: The various lawyers in your plays play different roles. In *A View from the Bridge,* the lawyer Alfieri is telling the story.

AM: He is also telling the hero that if he does what his emotions are moving him to do, he'll destroy himself. That lawyer is, you might even say, the rational principle, the principle of rationalizing one's life, and how limited it is once the emotions start to go. He's giving him all the reasons why he shouldn't be doing this.

MG: In *A View from the Bridge* the lawyer is somewhat removed from the immediate situation, whereas in *After the Fall* he is the protagonist. I wonder if he were not the protagonist, perhaps some greater flow of emotion — if not autobiography — might have been at work.

AM: The play was lambasted because there was too much auto-biography. That was the echo I got from the reviews. Rather than too little. I think what was missed completely because of the Marilyn connection was what the play was about. To me, that was the impulse for the play. When I started to write that play, Marilyn was alive. She wasn't dead. As far as I knew, she was perfectly OK. I didn't know the character was going to die. By the time I was halfway, two-thirds through, I realized there was no way out for this person.

MG: Did Marilyn die while you were writing the play?

AM: Yes. I was almost finished with it.

MG: But in the play she was dying.

AM: Oh, yeah. There was no way around it. But of course Marilyn herself had nearly died many times. I can't say that was a deep analysis of some sort.

MG: When you realized that the character in the play would have to die, was there a feeling that you yourself should take still another step in preventing the real person's death?

AM: [*quietly*] Couldn't. That's why she died. There was no way anyone...

She had the best analyst, Dr. [Ralph] Greenson. He went far beyond the normal professional relationship. She also had Dr. Marianne Kris, who was supposedly one of the great analysts. The point had arrived where I didn't know how to do that. That's the tragedy. There's no way to intervene at a certain point. [*emphatically*] A person's got to save himself. And sometimes you do and sometimes you don't.

MG: The theme of so many books and stories about Marilyn is: if only she had called me, I could have saved her.

AM: That's one of the attractions. Because she was so moving a person. Sure, everybody wants to do that, but some pretty devoted and, I think, able people couldn't do it.

MG: After she died, did you question yourself and wonder if there wasn't something you could have done?

AM: I did. But I couldn't. There was no way. She was beyond help. It's a failing in me, no doubt, but it is also a failing in every other human being she ever came in contact with, including, as I say, some of the most competent and devoted doctors. That's what tragedy is, and that's why it's so unacceptable most of the time. There's a denial of it that goes on. People deny that an *effect* has a cause.

MG: Inevitably people are going to think that a tragedy is irreversible.

AM: Theoretically it's possible to imagine that something can be reversed. But I'm afraid in reality our choices are very limited. It's not something you can just call up. That's the way it is. That's the way it is not only for ill people but for so-called healthy people who have to die, some of them when they never should have died, at the time when they're most productive and most wise — that seems a shame. But that's the way it is. I think it's a weakness of the civilization in a way that we create so much tragedy every day and deny its existence.

MG: Have you felt other times about other people that are close to you that there's an inevitability about it?

AM: Absolutely. Yes. Life is a struggle to overcome the inevitable. You can mitigate it, and we go on mitigating, and you're *obliged* to try to mitigate it, in my opinion. You can't simply passively accept bad circumstances. The amount of change that we're capable of is *vital*, but small. Nobody is an exception to this. This ameliorative philosophy where everybody is going to be capable of absolutely transforming his character, his nature, into a positive, wonderful personality — that's lollipop time. It has nothing to do with what's real, as far as I can tell.

MG: But each person can take responsibility for his life. To re-evoke your Mastroianni statement, with Marilyn, in a metaphorical if not an actual sense, you took a walk. You left. For the sake of your own sanity?

AM: There was simply nothing but destruction that could come, my own destruction, as well as hers. The point comes where you cannot continue anymore. There is no virtue in it, there is nothing positive, and your hope is that she can find some other means of saving herself. For me and anybody I knew it wasn't possible. Maybe there was a way in which she could do it.

MG: For you, it was a life-changing and life-seizing thing to leave.

AM: I spent five years trying to make that thing happen, and I couldn't. So, that's that.

MG: During the time you were with her, were you writing plays?

AM: Well, I did *The Misfits*, which took a *lot* of time, as any movie script does. You write it and you are involved in the production. That took about two and a half years. Before and after, I felt that the theatre didn't interest me. I couldn't get excited about it. I had written *A View from the Bridge* before this. I would probably never have written *A View from the Bridge* had I not been asked by Marty Ritt [Martin Ritt, later a film director], who was then an actor in a Broadway play called *The Flowering Peach* [by Clifford Odets], which Robert Whitehead produced. The play was failing. It had only x weeks to go, and they had a good cast, according to Marty. He called me up. I had never met him. He said, "We've got a theatre. We can use the theatre on Sunday nights. Do you have any one-act plays?" I said, "No I don't." He said, "We've got a wonderful group of actors here. We'd love to do something of yours, something we could do modestly." I said, "Well, there is one story that I've always wanted to write, but who the hell is going to put on a one-act play?" This was 1954 or 1955. The Off Broadway theatre was still in its youth, and it wasn't that easy to generate productions anyway. They had done *The Crucible* Off Broadway at the Martinique Theatre. That was, I think, one of the earliest such productions.

MG: At this point, you hadn't written *A View from the Bridge.*

AM: No. It was a one-act play in my mind. First I wrote *A Memory of Two Mondays.* Marty said, "Jesus, this would be wonderful, we can use up all our actors. Maybe you could do a curtain-raiser, because that only lasts an hour and 20 minutes, or something." Structurally, *A View from the Bridge* had one big arc, and it wasn't to be broken up into pieces. And I wrote that very rapidly. I gave it to him. So *A View from the Bridge* was going to be a curtain-raiser.

MG: Some curtain-raiser.

AM: Marty burst out laughing when he read it. He said, "Now what do we do?" In my mind, that was not written for Broadway. That was written for a theatre where people would do it in an impromptu sort of a way. As I said earlier, that's the way *Incident of Vichy* got written. Same idea. And incidentally the way a lot of music used to get written. The head of an orchestra would call up a composer and say, how about it, we've got a few good bugle players here.

MG: That isn't how plays usually get written.

AM: No! There's a disconnection there. But I'm convinced they used to get written that way. I would love to know, for example, the connection between Chekhov and Stanislavsky before he was turning out these plays.

MG: He might not have written the plays were it not for the Moscow Art Theatre?

AM: I wonder. I don't know.

MG: He was doing well with his short stories.

AM: Well, he was turning those out every couple of weeks. Pretty good stories. He didn't have to go into this monstrous business.

MG: And he failed with his first few plays.

AM: Why bother with the goddamn things? There must have been some outside stimulation. I believe in that — for certain writers. Now, a guy like O'Neill was so hermetic. The Provincetown Theatre was very instrumental in his work. He always had relations with directors, with Arthur Hopkins, with other such people who kept writing him notes.

MG: Have you had dry periods in your writing?

AM: Oh, I can go for a long time without being able to put anything down on paper. I'll always be writing scenes. I have hundreds of scenes, but whether they are plays or not is a different story. I discard them, and I've got endless notebooks. I make reference to them somewhat in my autobiography. See, a play to me is an integral piece of work, with a beginning, a middle and an end, whether it be a plot or simply a feeling. An anecdote is not enough. I have some structural sense that has to be satisfied. I will say that when I wrote *The Crucible* I realized suddenly how these Elizabethan guys could turn out the number of plays they did. It's such a simplistic idea, I don't know why it never occurred to me. They were all working off known stories. Shakespeare didn't invent any stories, except maybe for *Winter's Tale*, but even that is taken from something. See it's a great thing to be able to say, what's going to happen now, and pick up a history. And even if you don't use it, you see one road that you can move down, or discard. When I was doing *The Crucible,* I had an infinite number of story elements to choose from, or reject, or mold, or rework. I thought, Jesus, at this rate, you can do a play every three months!

MG: Having discovered that, with the exception of *The Creation of the World,* you didn't do it again.

AM: No. I don't know why.

MG: People assume that *Salesman* was very personal, they assume that through a certain transposition of time, *The Crucible* was also, and *After the Fall* because of the auto-biographical elements. But other than that, people don't know. Was *The Price* direct from life?

AM: Well, it's not *me*. But the fratricide that goes on in a lot of these plays, the brother conflict...

MG: You had a brother conflict?

AM: You got a brother?

MG: Yes.

AM: How else can you have a brother? Look at *Salesman.* There are a pair of brothers who adore one another and also are at odds.

MG: Do brothers go through the plays?

AM: Well, in *Creation of the World,* there are fellas named Cain and Abel. [*laughs*] That's a family play. And *The Price,* of course. I don't think I would ever do that again. I haven't done it in many years, using the family that way.

MG: Is *The Price* the closest to your own family?

AM: It isn't really. It was based on other people. Actually I get along very well with my brother. But one lives on a metaphorical level as well as a real one. Everybody thought I was killing my father in that play. Quite the contrary. I never had a cross word with him.

99

MG: Then what are the personal elements in the plays?

AM: I don't know how to phrase it. There are obviously certain elements that get repeated, that family I refer to, with a father-son business. I saw a production of *All My Sons* in England, directed by Michael Blakemore, with Rosemary Harris and Colin Blakely. And nobody like Rosemary Harris had ever played that part, except once in, of all places, Jerusalem, where I happened to be when it was playing. In Jerusalem, as in London, a marvelous juicy actress, the one who got her leg shot off in the Munich Olympics. She was fantastically *there*, as was Rosemary Harris. Suddenly I looked at this. I had completely forgotten. The original title of that play was *The Sign of the Archer*. *The Sign of the Archer* had to do with the sign under which that son was born, and later he was the one who got killed, or killed himself. I realized watching the production in England that she had been the center of that thing when I started.

MG: The wife?

AM: Yes. The mother. And Rosemary and Blakemore in London knew nothing of the history of the productions of that play and the movie, which emphasized Eddie [Edward G.] Robinson and Burt Lancaster and Arthur Kennedy and so on. Rosemary and Blakemore didn't assume at all that the basic thing was a father and son play. They assumed something quite different, which my original title assumed, that when the curtain goes up, the wife knows the whole story. And Rosemary played it as though she knows it. There's a kind of vengeance in that play by her on that man, the father, the husband, which is quite a different emphasis.

The woman has it within herself, quietly and without demonstration, to be a survivor. That interests me. In London I looked at the play quite differently than I had before. In *Bridge*, there's a similar thing. The women know more. They're less obsessional. The men are obsessed. The women have to preserve that nest. They're a very conservative force. That production in England really made me think, how I had gotten misled. The mother's obsessed with the stars. What had I changed the title to? *All My Sons.* It completely altered the central emphasis of the play.

MG: But wouldn't the audience still come out with the feeling that it's about the father and *All My Sons*?

AM: Yes, excepting that with Rosemary Harris, it wasn't simply narrowed down to that conflict. She created an ambience there that you could cut with a knife. It was quite wonderful. It was far more interesting to me.

MG: It's curious how much a title affects a public understanding of a play.

AM: It tells you what to look for.

MG: What if *Death of a Salesman* had a different title?

AM: In China for example, Zhu Lin is the woman who played Linda Loman, and she plays queens, princesses, powerful political figures in traditional Chinese plays. I saw her in one: tremendous grandeur. I talked to her, and I said, "How do you see this play [*Salesman*]?" She said, "There are still women like this in China." I said, "In other words you think she's quite manipulatable, and she's following behind Willy." She said, "Yes." I said, "That's not the way it is at all," and I gave her some cues, and it was interesting to watch. That's the woman who tells the sons, look he's going to kill himself. She knows the story. Once she caught on to that, Willy gets bigger, it makes everything bigger. Funny though, what interested me when I told her that and I saw the difference, I thought why is it nobody sees that? Anywhere. They all think Linda is sort of a wet rag. The lines aren't that way. She's got great indignation and wrath! She's tough. With him, she's got to maneuver and manipulate him. She can't confront him because he'd wipe her out. I wonder if the father-son business again sucked out all the energy.

MG: To go back a bit, could you talk about what you think is the subjectivity of the plays?

AM: What is subjectivity? I can't define it. I can't work simply out of knowing something. I could never have written *The Crucible* simply because I wanted to write a play about the blacklisting.

MG: Or a play about the real events in Salem?

AM: Never. The center of that play is the guilt of John Proctor, and the working out of that guilt. Indeed it finally exemplifies the guilt of man in general. I believe in a seamless linking of the internal life of the person with the social situation. You can't have a witch hunt over a period of time in a society that is not walking around riddled with guilt. The witch hunt and the Red hunt strummed the chords of guilt in people and made them the willing victims or its collaborators. McCarthy spoke of the New Deal as 20 years of treason. He wasn't talking about Communism. He was talking about the New Deal, until finally I thought there were certain words that people weren't using as much, the idea of revolution, organization, group — they could be very incendiary compositions. I suppose he was playing on a guilt which I can transfer even to sexual matters. It's the hidden enemy. It's subconscious and to exculpate that it hardly matters what the subject is.

The Chinese were the same way. The Chinese were probably the best single exposition of this. They literally would sit somebody down and have what they call a struggle meeting with them. What does that mean? Any secret idea he may have had, however remotely connected to social events, which was not an expression of willingness to give over his personality to a society, was the footprint of the enemy. In effect they would psychoanalyze somebody. And it took a person of extraordinary strength to deny his guilt, to deny that he had guilt. Nien Cheng is one of the few to have that strength and one of the reasons she had it was because she was an aristocrat. She did not come into the situation as a democrat. She came in with certain perceptions about society, namely that there are those more or less fit to govern, more and less able to succeed. The leveling idea had never been part of her life. You get somebody through some ideology or another that they do believe everybody is equal then it is a matter of guilt if it turns out that you really don't believe that.

The conversation continued over lunch, and Inge Morath joined us.

MG: You said the other day that there was something you used to do outside that had become more difficult...

AM: There are certain walks you take over a period of years, coming up the same hill you realize you're not coming up quite the way as you used to come up. But I'm in pretty good shape. I can't complain.

IM: You come up a lot better than when you used to smoke so much.

MG: Did you smoke a lot?

AM: Yes. I would inhale a pipe and cigars. Now that I think of it, it was unbelievable. When I would sit in my studio out there, which is a twelve-by-fourteen building, I realize now what I was doing to myself; I would fill it full of smoke and in the winter time with the windows closed. More than once, I got dizzy. I had vertigo. I had to open the door and walk outside and go back in and smoke some more. But I recovered and if you recovered, it can't be so bad.

MG: Do you exercise every day?

AM: I don't do as much as I should, but I have a rowing machine upstairs and a bicycle and I try to walk. We just spent a week in Barbados where you get up in the morning and walk down to the beach and swim for 20 minutes. Then you do that a couple of times a day, which makes me realize how little exercise I'm doing. I split a lot of wood, which is terrific. That's real good exercise. You breathe deeply as well as lift and move your muscles, tighten up your belly. It's the breathing, that's the thing. I like the breathing that comes as a result of effort, not just sitting there breathing.

MG: In New York, when I asked you if you had any bad habits, you said, yes, wasting time, specifically reading *The New York Times*.

AM: I got rid of the worst thing that I did, which was killing me, and that was the smoking. I would have been dead by now. I never had a pipe out of my mouth. I would go to the dentist and he would look in my mouth and say, "Well, you've got the pre-cancer situation." It was really the end of the road.

MG: And suddenly you stopped?

AM: One morning. I had tried 50 different times but I couldn't do it. I did it one morning, as a result of a tremendous revelation that came to me. You see, I had a routine. I would go up to the studio after breakfast and light a pipe. One morning I forgot to light the pipe. 20 minutes had passed after the normal juncture at which I would light the pipe. This had happened before and when it did happen I would immediately reach for the pipe and light it. This time when I reached for the pipe I realized that I didn't want to smoke. What I had was a fear that I would lose the habit. It had never been so clear to me. I thought, well I'm going to smoke when I feel like it, not when I'm afraid I'm going to lose the habit. And that's going to happen in five minutes. I went back to work and about a half hour later I realized I hadn't smoked yet this morning. In that morning I had perhaps one real urgent desire to smoke. It was now 11:30. Normally I would have lit four or five pipes. So if I could defeat just one real desire to smoke, this is within reason. With no faith whatsoever that I was going to succeed, I went through the day without smoking. The next day was easier because I probably had less poison in me. That poison is an irritant which makes you want one more. That's the last time I smoked. The reason I didn't make anything of it is that I had no faith in it. Before I would moralistically talk to myself, give myself all kinds of lectures the way everybody does who smokes. Never worked. It was purely a separation of one impulse from another. One impulse was the desire to smoke, the other was that if you didn't smoke now, you might not really want to smoke.

MG: In the early days, did the smoking fuel the writing?

AM: Shakespeare never smoked.

MG: How do we know?

AM: If he did, Raleigh handed him a pipe every now and then. In fact, it was unheard of when I was a kid. Very few people I experienced would carry cigarettes in their pockets, even smokers. You didn't walk around in the street smoking cigarettes. It would be something you would relax with. I had uncles who smoked. But you didn't carry cigarettes. It would be the equivalent of carrying a bottle of whisky in your pocket. Very strange behavior. Then they started these campaigns: reach for a Lucky instead of a sweet. That was the slogan. I don't drink a lot. I do drink some.

MG: Did you ever?

AM: No.

IM: I don't think your work depends on this kind of stimulus at all.

AM: I know a lot of writers who either stopped smoking, or never smoked. Bellow did once.

MG: Certainly there are writers who are fuelled by drinking or smoking.

AM: Yes. Those who were injured by alcohol would say, you lost as much as you gave, in terms of debilitation and energy. What about the great novelists? I wonder about Dickens. I don't know what his intake of stimulants was.

MG: I can't imagine that Dickens or Balzac would have had time to take anything. They were creating every second of the day.

IM: Balzac drank too much coffee. He killed himself.

MG: Artists today, if they can't create, may be driven to something else. When you can't write, what do you do — since you're not a drinker or smoker? You just take a walk?

AM: I do a lot of woodwork. I build things like the table you're eating on now. And the big dining-room table in there and all this furniture. I drive myself crazy doing that. Split wood and annoy my wife.

MG: And that gets the creative juices going?

AM: I wish I knew what gets me going. More than anything I would guess is a sudden joy in hearing some kind of language that gets me excited. You see, I'm part mime. I used to be able to do any kind of accent, except Danish. It's the only language nobody ever gets, except Victor Borge, who is Danish. They do clicks.

IM: He does Chinese pretty well.

AM: I can do Chinese. What is it that Chinese professor at Columbia says: "coochural" [cultural]? "American coochure." The l's are a problem in the middle of a word. When I was directing *Salesman* [in China], I could tell when they were wrong in their readings even though they were speaking Chinese. The first time they did that, I said, "You're being very sentimental there." And they really got nervous. I could tell after going through three rehearsals of the same scene.

When I saw *View from the Bridge* in Russia, back in 1960, I knew immediately they had screwed around with the text. I know no Russian but I could tell from the relationships that they had jumped various parts of the script. They admitted that. In the case of *View from the Bridge*, I never knew those people [the Italians in the play], but I spent time in Italy after World War II and I love the way the Italians speak English. I had gone to high school and grammar school with a lot of Italian kids, so that the lingo was in my head. I had been told some of the story, the fundamentals of the story, long before, and it always struck me how Greek that story was. It was a Greek tale, but how to do that?

Then I saw Ulu's production [Ulu Grosbard] of the play with [Robert] Duvall, which was a phenomenal piece of work, really a great production. Watching it, I realized that down deep was a whole story of incest. The incestuous expression came out of some deep recess of my head; I was totally unaware of it. Without that, I wonder if I would have written the damn thing. I'm sure now people don't think of it in those terms. I did, but only when I saw it five years after I had written it.

MG: People do think of that.

AM: And yet there is no incest in it. She's not his daughter.

MG: Symbolically she is.

AM: It must mean that I laid it in as though she were.

IM: The Italians love that play.

AM: I went down to see it again and by this time Duvall had left and [Richard] Castellano was in it. If you recall that open stage practically ran into the orchestra, so that the actors were looking right into the faces in the audience. Castellano said, "One night I looked out and there was this guy, he looked an Italian laborer and he was in tears. He was the last one to leave the theatre. We were taking bows, and from the back of that theatre I watched this guy because he was so overwhelmed. Two days later he was back in his seat. Again he was overwhelmed. He came three times and the third time, I thought I would find out about him. At the end, we took our bows and everybody left and this guy was staggering out." So Castellano went up to him and spoke in Italian and the man said, "I know this family, in the Bronx." He said the whole story is true, except for one thing, the end. He said, "Eddie took a nap and the boy came in and stabbed him."

Alternative ending. It's like *A Doll's House*. For Nora to leave was unthinkable in Germany. Ibsen wrote an ending in which she didn't go. She stayed. That's a version they played in his lifetime. It was simply too much for them.

MG: That sounds like all the variant versions of *King Lear* after Shakespeare died.

AM: I wrote a radio play about that. That's William Ireland's version. William Ireland was a young boy in the time of Richard Brinsley Sheridan. His father was a book collector and a professional antique guy. He was an illegitimate son, so he lived in the basement. Chatterton had been a famous forger of poetry, and was his god. They got him a job in a law office as a very minor clerk, and he would wander through the bookstores, and quite by chance he came across a prayer book that had belonged to Queen Whatever. He brought it home and his father asked where he found it. For the first time, he was noticed by his father and was brought up to sit at the table for dinner with these great worthies of British culture. The kid got very excited. His father said, keep it up, if you see any other things, let me know. The son had become very good at copying handwriting. To make a long story short, he decided to discover something else, and he discovered a letter from Shakespeare to his wife and brought it home, and watched his father look at it. He went to some experts on handwriting and they said there's no doubt about it — including the paper.

The father asked, "Where did you get this?" The son said, "I was walking along and this carriage knocked me down. A great gentleman got out, picked me up and took me home and he gave me something to eat. He asked who I was and I said I was your son. He said he had a trunkful of Elizabethan documents, which he allowed me to look at. He asked me not to tell you about this because he did not want the notoriety. But he said he was going to let me take home a few things, from time to time." He called him Mr. H. The next thing was a copied sonnet. Now the kid is the celebrated center of conversation at every dinner, and he's accepted by his father, so he has to keep on producing. Now he's going to give him the original copy of *King*

Lear.

At the time, the Puritan attitude was getting stronger and stronger. He finally produced this manuscript, and first of all it had a happy ending. Secondly, he removed from it all the violence of language, which curses out heaven, the rough language which indicates anything more than a kind of friendly attitude among the people. He laundered the play, and it took him a while. He brings it home, his father looks at it. He brings in Boswell and a critic, [Edmond] Malone, who worked on original manuscripts. He had quite a circle of people and they all sat around while a reading was given of this play. Meanwhile its validity was almost beyond question because he had produced this other stuff.

Boswell got to his knees before the manuscript and said, "Forgive us, dear Bard, for all our transgressions against the beauty of your manuscript, fouled by these vile actors. Now we have purely *Lear*." The Prince of Wales was charmed. Sheridan said he would put it on soon. When that reading was over, the kid couldn't be restrained. He said, "Mr. H. has promised me a hitherto unknown play."

Months later he comes in with a five act tragedy and this is read and Sheridan says, "I will put it on." At which point, Malone said, "It's all a fraud. Shakespeare could never have written this piece of garbage." Well, they threw Malone out of the club immediately. [*laughs*] He was spoiling everything. So they put the play on and Sheridan directed it and some of their best actors were in it. At the end of act one or act two, there were like 26 dead bodies on stage. Malone had organized a claque. They began to hoot and howl and everybody realized after watching this performance that it was simply absurd. They got the kid in the green room because now all these famous lords had put themselves on the line. Their expertise guaranteed this work, and they collared him and rammed him up against the wall and said, "Who is Mr. H.?" "He has agreed to appear, tomorrow evening at my father's house at five o'clock." At five o'clock, a carriage drives up and out gets this gentleman, and he goes in the house. That's the end of the story. Nobody knows what happened to Ireland. The theories are that he ran off with the servant girl whom he was living with in the basement. It was the scandal of the period.

MG: One thing it proves: occasionally critics can be right.

AM: [*laughs*] Or they can be wrong for a very long time. I made a radio play out of it. It's called *William Ireland's Confession.*

MG: Would you ever want to turn that into a stage play?

AM: There's no good reason excepting I suppose it seems so obvious to me. It should be a farce. By the time the kid comes in with the second document, you've got to know more than the father knows. His innocence is far too stupefying. Its very predictability should be its comedy.

MG: It would give you a chance to write a comedy.

AM: Well, things may come to that. I love that story. It's such a delight. It would be a wonderful movie. I'm amazed no one has done it. The basic psychological truth of it is his fantasy in both trying to be accepted by his father and to destroy him. Implicit in that was a tricking. If the boy were merely trying to be accepted, he would have stopped early. But of course the father was asking for destruction. Every time, he would say, "Well, produce something."

MG: It has all your father and son themes. Do you think somewhere someone is inventing an Arthur Miller play?

AM: I'm sure they have already. More than one. That was one of my impulses for writing my autobiography because at least I want my version in circulation.

MG: When did you begin writing it?

AM: I think I really began many years ago. I would start reminiscences, which I would give to Aaron Asher [his editor] and then I wouldn't write any more. Then he would ask me for more and I would give him another 20 pages. In the end, I never used any of that.

IM: Then people would come who want to write about you.

AM: My hair would stand up. I would realize this was inevitable.

MG: How would you respond to people who want to write a biography of you?

AM: I wouldn't want it, because, for me to sit down and talk about my life — I can write it three times during the time it would take me to tell it. And it would never come out right anyway.

MG: In the 1940s and 1950s, there was an active Broadway theatre. But not today. Why is that?

AM: I'll tell you what I really think. I think that we arrived at a certain point — historically. Once there was one audience in New York. The same guy who went to see O'Neill went to see the *Ziegfeld Follies*. The idea that there were two or more distinct audiences was not there. The only such distinction that I ever was conscious of, possibly, was when the Group Theatre was going. It was only a matter of perhaps five years when it was really producing stuff: you had a kind of left-wing audience. That was the only time I was conscious there was a split in the audience.

MG: Did the same audience go to see *Salesman, Streetcar,* and *Oklahoma*?

AM: Oh, absolutely. As a consequence of that, one approached writing a play with no thought that there was going to be the support of a clique, that is, an aesthetic clique, a political clique, a group of like-minded people. So your play had to extend its embrace to every kind of person that would be interested in going to the theatre. He could be a dentist or a professor or a student. He could be on the left, he could be on the right.

MG: But a play can't be all things to all people.

AM: Of course, it can't be, but the assumption on the part of the writer, the director and the actors was that the material was available to every man or woman. What happened sometime, I would place it maybe 1954, 1955, 1956, I became conscious that there was an alienation in one part of the audience, which was fatal. Tennessee was still producing work, and I was, but the feeling was that "there was nothing to see." About this time, the Off Broadway theatre began to become fairly active. It was nothing like what it would become, but for the first time you heard about Paul Libin who did that production of *The Crucible* at the Martinique which was part of the McAlpine Hotel. The idea of creating a new environment, that was a new thing. What I'm driving at is that if you're writing a play and you cannot rely upon the support of like-minded folks, you've got to prove the story in a different way. You can't make assertions based on some cultural unity. You've got to make it explain itself all the time. The result was that you got larger stories, stories that would carry a person from point A to point F. They would not be satisfied sitting there and listening to some talk. It activated our theatre. When I went to Europe, the first time in 1947, I was struck by one thing: the verbalization of theatre in Europe, the comparative lack of action. I saw *Ondine* [by Jean Giraudoux] in Paris in 1947, and I know enough French to know what was happening there. This was a popular play, with [Louis] Jouvet. He sat in this chair for fifteen minutes talking to this wraith, and the story was going nowhere. It was motionless.

MG: But it played in New York. Giraudoux, Anouilh, Eliot were all done on Broadway.

AM: Listen, they played it, but put it this way: if an American playwright had the success of Giraudoux in New York, he would be called a failure. I saw *The Madwoman of Chaillot* [by Giraudoux]. It was absolutely marvelous. But I don't think it ran that long. In those times, you were a success if you ran at least two seasons.

MG: The next wave of serious playwriting came Off Broadway: Edward Albee, Arthur Kopit, Jack Gelber — and only Albee was successful on Broadway.

AM: And Albee was always essentially a non-Broadway writer, though *Virginia Woolf* happened to be successful there. My point is that the relationship to the audience was very different. Past that nebulous point, the audience was atomized. The most hip, the most sophisticated was drawn away, the less sophisticated, the squarer audience remained.

MG: The more sophisticated went to the movies as well as Off Broadway. Art movies came along.

AM: Yes. About 1947 or 1948, neo-realism started in Italy. This man was running a little business, the World Theatre, and was regarded as a daring entrepreneur to bring in these pictures with subtitles, no less. *The Bicycle Thief* and *Open City* and so forth. That kind of sophistication began. When I was a student in the 1930s, I would go to the art cinema league, an organization on campus, and we brought in foreign pictures, but it was regarded as a very arcane thing to see a picture that wasn't made in America — even to most intellectuals. It wasn't an art form yet.

In France, there was a boulevard theatre, like our Broadway. There was also Sartre, with *Huis Clos* and maybe *Caligula* [by Albert Camus]. They were separate theatres. The bourgeoise did go to both. I noticed that in the boulevard theatre there was an atmosphere of the expensive restaurants. I was in England in 1957 when Peter Brook did *A View from the Bridge*. There was a big mass meeting at the Royal Court Theatre. I was on the platform with five or six others, all English. The question came up: how come the American theatres had such vitality and the British theatre was so stultified? There was one play: *Look Back in Anger*, which had opened three or four months before this meeting.

The homogenized audience, the unified audience was breaking up somewhere around the same period. In England, the solution to the problem was a subsidized theatre: the Old Vic, numerous others, based on an earlier tradition they had. With us, the playwright was confronted with the Off Broadway situation. Only rarely could he hope to make a living because of the size of those houses. In England, he wouldn't get rich on the National Theatre, but its impact on the culture was far greater. He had access to great stars, accomplished actors. Most of our Off Broadway plays were done, I think, by much younger people, not yet proven.

In the 1940s and the early half of the 1950s I think you were receiving a stimulus from the audience. You did get the illusion, although I used to complain even then that we had a very fragmentary audience. In fact, I wrote an article for the Times saying that ordinary people could not get to the theatre for whatever reason. It was an upper-middle-class audience, but nevertheless it was a far broader audience. An excitement came out of the feeling that you were talking to the country. I always suspected that it was an illusion. You only had to go to the movies to see another audience. You never saw a black person in the Broadway theatre.

AM: I was just in England. For a play like *The Archbishop's Ceiling*, they have an extraordinary group of accomplished actors. The young man playing the lead, Roger Allam, left a big hit to go into this. I asked him and he said, "I thought it would be interesting." What an answer! He felt that he had at his disposal certain choices. This thing is only going to run until March. With *American Clock* there must have been twenty actors plus a live orchestra on stage. There's a certain kind of playfulness in the audience. Maybe it's because they're younger or maybe it's because they didn't pay $40 to get in. It has to do with the environment. Different environments create different emotions, and in this particular one, you get the feeling they're open, they're interested, they're not there for some ancillary reason.

AM: In writing my book [*Timebends*], I got very discouraged about history, not that I had many illusions about it. But history is a story. I tell a story in a certain way. I have a viewpoint toward a lot of events, but there are numerous other ways to treat the same material. What's real? Well, you are real in relation to that object, to that event. The event as I tell it is tempered by me. Who am I?

MG: When you finish your autobiography, what you say will be regarded as the truth.

AM: As far as I know, but another guy can come in and say, well, look, I was there and it's all different.

MG: Then you have the case of Lillian Hellman. People say that what she said in her memoirs wasn't true.

AM: She became involved with writing fiction and putting it in the first person.

MG: Your autobiography is all true?

AM: I hope so. I was at the Chicago convention in 1968 [the Democratic National Convention]. I was a delegate from the town of Roxbury, so I was sitting on the floor. I was aware of what was going on outside, as many delegates were. On television screens you could see where the cops were hitting the kids. But I could see where delegates could go through the same experience and think that was a minor detail. The main thing was that Humphrey got nominated.

MG: In your book, you're obviously trying to set the record straight about many things.

AM: It's not so much setting the record straight. A lot of it is told for the first time. For instance, there's a whole section on postwar Europe that I was involved in. I was in Italy in 1947 when it was generally thought that Italy was going to become a communist state, just before the big national election.

MG: What were you doing there?

AM: I just wanted to see what was happening in Europe. I had not been in the war and I had never been to Europe before. A man I knew [Vincent Longhi] was trying to run for Congress. His idea was to go to Calabria in Sicily and visit the homes of immigrants, people who came here. I thought, here's my chance. I spent about a month in Europe. It was very meaningful. So it's not setting the record straight. It's my life, my times — I saw it.

MG: In terms of setting the record straight, I would think that one area would be your relationship with Kazan, the ambiguities of that relationship.

AM: There remain ambiguities. There'll always be. Bob Anderson [the playwright Robert Anderson] told me that Kazan had to redo a lot of his book [A Life] because his publisher wanted certain things. Whatever's vital in my life, I hope is there in my book, but it's a big life and I can't cover everything. It's a hard thing to do, because a lot is interesting only to me. I think there is some insight into the time. It's basically a mystery, of how theatre changed. I know it changed. I know some of the symptoms of how it changed, but it's beyond me to tell you why.

MG: If you had been coming out of college fifteen or twenty years later, you might not have gone into the theatre. You might have been a novelist.

AM: It's questionable. The simplistic idea that writing, especially writing for the theatre, is an autonomous act, can't be supported. When I was coming up in the 1930s, the theatre for some reason was seized upon by the left as an exciting art form. Odets was a terrific dynamic image. And the Group Theatre was. And there were others. Eva Le Gallienne was going then. You could see Ibsen as a social critic. At the time, society was *the* subject. It was in crisis. You couldn't sit down with anybody, no matter what his viewpoint was, without talking about Roosevelt. What's going to happen next? When is the unemployment going to go down? The theatre became an extremely exciting thing for a young writer. Hundreds of people walking around trying to write plays about this moment, this hour. I was a carryover from that, and I'm convinced that Tennessee was. As a response to society, it's the movies that have dealt with the big social problems. You see, the movies turn it into a social problem. I've never dealt with social problems. I'm dealing with a moral question of a human being in a society. If I were dealing with social problems, you wouldn't be looking at *The Crucible* today. And it is being looked at all over the world.

MG: You're a moralist playwright rather than a social one?

AM: I suppose that's true. I'm not drawing morals. It's just that man is a moral creature. He's either fighting it or he's with it or he has an ambiguous relationship with it, but it's always there. If I may say so, I think that's why these plays have not faded with the problems they dealt with.

MG: In the same way, would you say that Ibsen was a moralist playwright?

AM: Yes. And he was my inspiration for a long time. Take a thing like *An Enemy of the People*, which is his most poster-type play. The man in that play couldn't help it. It's a philosophical, moral problem, namely how much right does an individual have to contradict the beliefs and sense of reality of a society? In that play, he went so far as to say, the majority is always wrong. And that in nature, in the world of biology there are higher and lower species. That's why some people thought the character was fascist, and why he finally made a speech to a trade union group saying he was not an elitist in that sense. What he was trying to say was that there was a greater or lesser degree of sensitivity to the question of accepting given truths.

MG: Would you go as far as Ibsen in saying that the majority is always wrong?

AM: I think so. What he meant basically was by the time they are on to an idea, it probably has begun to cease to be true.

MG: In dealing with venereal disease in *Ghosts*, the problems may have faded.

AM: However, if you do *Ghosts* now and talk about inherited character failings or inherited spiritual damage, which is what derived from the idea of syphilis, it gets a little ridiculous — until you can discount their relative ignorance about the way that disease is transmitted. Occasionally, he stepped over the boundary and made it a little too much of a medical and social problem.

MG: In reviewing a biography of Strindberg, you expressed a kinship with him. I was not aware of that connection.

AM: He meant a hell of a lot to me. You see there were so many Strindbergs, partly because his whole personality was being shattered and put together again. There was no question about it: he was as crazy as could be. I could identify five or six different Strindbergs. The misogynist is pathological. I couldn't identify with that. But there's another part of him that has to do with the vision of the inexorability of the tragic circumstance, that once a destructive apparatus gets into motion, it's almost impossible to stop it. I can relate to that. Once that is really moving — get out of the way. The structure of his plays is based on that vision. The trouble is that so much of him is just…sick. It comes out as sickness. I can't relate to that. Inevitably he hated Ibsen as being fundamentally somebody who had collapsed in front of the bourgeois demands upon him. But Ibsen had Strindberg's picture over his desk, because there's a truthteller in him.

MG: Could you choose between the two? Which one is more important to you?

AM: I can't. Ibsen is far more invulnerable. He protected his flanks all the time. He was far more political. Strindberg would damage himself. It would never occur to him to shave something or to protect himself. Occasionally when he was in the middle of one of his so-called "swings," as he veered toward center he would get a little careful and kid the reader a little bit. But not for long. I put it in terms of power. Ibsen was one of those philosophers who was trying to run the world. He wanted to change society. Strindberg also wanted to, but in a way that would require such a revolting confrontation with perversity, that effectively it was impossible. I read him the same time I read Ibsen. What I got from him is what you get from some of the Greek plays, that when Fate begins to move, it may take a long time, but it will get you in the end.

MG: You do want to change things with your plays, don't you?

AM: Sure. That's implicit in them. In *All My Sons,* I was dealing with corruption involving twenty fliers and a few tens of thousands of dollars worth of stuff — well, this is child's play now. If you say, do you want to change things? I could die laughing. A change from terrible to impossible! Look at the number of people who have been sent away to prison for violations of regulations in relation to war production. Profiteering and so forth and so on. If anything, our sensitivity toward this has increased since *All My Sons.*

MG: Do you ever think about what your legacy would be?

AM: [*quickly*] Some good parts for actors.

MG: Some good parts for actors?

AM: This is not said speciously. I look at the plays that I've done, that is those plays that continue to have their life, and if you look hard enough you're going to find that they've got pretty good parts for actors. Now there are exceptions. But actors and directors have got to decide to do these plays. They're not deciding because the play has quote-unquote great moral importance. Even *literary* importance. They're deciding because they've got a hell of an idea of how to do this part. Look at a play that never ceases to be done. With the long nose. What is that about? Does anybody really believe in that romance anymore? But there's a fantastic role there for a romantic type actor. When does he get a chance to do that? So one after another rises to his maturity and says, "I'm going to play that guy." Similarly with Shakespeare, it would be interesting to find out which of the plays is done most, in terms of numbers of performances. I don't know but I would be inclined to think it would be the ones with the big interesting central parts.

I think Willy Loman is going to be around a long time because that's a challenge. You can do it in a number of different ways. And it takes a big actor to do it. An actor of lesser capacity is going to fail. That production of *View from the Bridge* with Michael Gambon. Now, why is he doing it? It has to be that he looked at that and said, "Now I can do that the way no one else has done that." If periodically people keep doing that, that means those plays will last.

MG: Do you want your epitaph to be: "He gave good parts to actors?"

AM: I wouldn't mind! There are lesser things you can do with your life. I would hope that there would be more seen in them, that they are an image of some kind of the human circumstance. But I think that offering good parts goes with it. There are probably a lot of good parts in very inferior work, which don't get done. I think there's a limit to the truth of that statement, but I think you have to have that in order for the thing to live. And why not? After all, it's an art where the actor is expressing himself as well as the author and the director.

MG: What that statement doesn't do is distinguish you from other playwrights. Tennessee could have said the same thing, and in fact it's true. Obviously actresses will always want to play Blanche.

AM: There is another element, of course. I'm too modest to say what it is. My plays are dealing with essential dilemmas of what it means to be human. I would hope they are, anyway.

MG: There are cycles. You're evidently going through a revival. Wherever you turn, you see yourself. There has to be a reason for that — not just good parts for actors.

AM: I wondered about that the other day and I wondered whether a point had come where these plays had detached themselves from their time. They're now freewheeling.

MG: They're out there in space somewhere?

AM: Yeah, they're out there in space now. They're what we call [*laughs*] artworks. I'll never forget sitting in a theatre when Olivier directed *The Crucible* in the 1960s. Inge and I were sitting there. Positively marvelous production. At the Old Vic, I guess it was. A woman in front of us turned to her companion at the intermission and said, "Didn't this have something to do with what's-his-name, that senator?" I thought, it's like being born again. The point would come when nobody would remember McCarthy's name. It's like seeing Essex and Elizabeth in a play and saying, "Now what was that story again?" You've got to remember that this was Essex and Elizabeth in their time. That was the big shocker! That was the most important statement being made in England, and who the hell remembers it?

MG: Is the revival of your work like being born again?

AM: I feel terrific about it because obviously it makes you feel you haven't lived in vain, and furthermore the so-called Broadway theatre is not the theatre. By February, I will have three plays running at the same time in London and not one play in New York, except the one-acts at Lincoln Center. And I say, that's the way it should be. Because those three plays are in the subsidized National Theatre and the Royal Shakespeare Company, and that's where I belong.

MG: And during the same time there will be productions of *Salesman* and *The Crucible* around the country.

121

AM: They're going on now, they're going on all the time. But not in New York. I say to myself, OK, if that's happening to me, what does that say about what it's doing to the new, unknown or the hardly-known writers, who are thinking in some misconceived part of their brains of aiming their career toward a profession of playwriting. It's absolutely killing. It's a marginal occupation.

MG: It wasn't always.

AM: It was not. And I still say, under the right circumstances, every theatre in the so-called Broadway area could be full within two or three years, if the price of tickets was brought down and a couple of other things were done. This is not some natural consequence. This is a result of a certain set of sociological courses which can be remedied.

MG: Even if they were remedied there is a question whether the playwrights would be there — and if the actors would be there to do the plays.

AM: Well, then you would have to start from that. Look, I have these two short plays [*I Can't Remember Anything* and *Clara*]. Those four actors seem to be as good as anybody you'd want. They're as good as anybody in England. I think we're richer than that goddamn situation on Broadway allows us to be.

MG: Recently you had a one-act performed by Wallace Shawn.

AM: That was not a play. I had my pocket picked on a bus on First Avenue and I wrote a little piece of prose about it, which I didn't bother to try to get published. A man sat down near me, looked like he had just come out of a hospital. He kept writhing in his seat, looking very uncomfortable. He picked my pocket while he was doing that. I wrote a sort of half-wry thing. Wally read it. I wasn't there to hear him read it. People told me it was wonderful. He's a very good performer. The whole thing was in first person, and his wryness must have been terrific in it.

MG: Last January we had that panel of playwrights, and we talked too little about the creative process.

AM: A writer talking about his work is unable to talk about the center of it, which is the obsessional part of it, because if he talked about it, it wouldn't be obsessional anymore. That's the part: you can't see your own ears. You look in a mirror and you see your eyes, and if you look at your ears you don't see your eyes. You can't look at them both at the same time. And that's the part: you can't look at it.

The phone rings. It's the playwright Honor Moore, who lives nearby.

MG: Many writers and artists live near here.

AM: When I moved here, there was me and Alexander Calder. It was all farms, every house here but ours.

MG: And now?

AM: I'm trying to think of the farms. I know two and there are probably another six. It's become one of those semi-suburban areas. The economics editor of *Time* lives here, and he has a computer tied into the telephone. He showed me how it works.

MG: Do you have a computer?

AM: I work on a word processor now. I wrote this book [*Timebends*] on it, only because when I got through about 250 pages and realized the size of this thing, I thought I was going to drown in paper. Honor was the one who sold me. I went through hell learning how to use it. I was ready to throw it out fifteen times. Now I'm very good at it.

MG: Have you written a play on it yet?

AM: No. I wrote a 150-page outline for a television version of *The American Clock* on it.

MG: As you know, I've just been talking to Martha Clarke. Her work, combining dance and theatre and extraordinary visual images, is so very different from yours.

AM: Well, you know there's drama and there's theatre, and they're not necessarily the same thing. It's neither better nor worse, just two different beasts happen to be taking place on the stage. My concept — I didn't invent it — the idea of a play being the story of birds coming home to roost, which is basically the classical theatre. That's gone by the boards. Plays today are incidents, not a long articulated arch where the past is being grappled with.

MG: That's still true in your work, even in the one-acts. They're memory plays.

AM: I can't wait to see what an audience makes of those. I've often said this: there are very few playwrights that stay in the theatre as long as I have. There are some others. Beckett is another one. But for the most part, it's a young man's game. Maugham was very successful; he left. A lot of people left.

MG: How long have you been in the theatre?

AM: Really I started writing plays in the 1930s, but I didn't get produced until the 1940s. I've been obsessed with it all that time. That's a long time to be obsessed with the same thing, but I can see why. You throw yourself at the mercy of actors.

MG: And also directors.

AM: And directors. And the weather.

MG: And then the critics.

AM: Critics are the least of it. I've never really been surprised by critics.

MG: What's kept you going for so many years?

AM: An unanswered question. I don't know. You get a vision of a form, which is almost like a building or a structure like a tree, and you are compelled to complete that form, to literally make it. Like that table in there, that dining-room table that I built. It's not unlike it. You can envisage an object. If you have the technique or the talent, if you can think of it, you can make it.

MG: With a carpenter, at a certain point his tables get better and better. He knows more about what he is doing. In a sense, you started out with *Death of a Salesman*.

AM: It was about my tenth play.

MG: It was your third on Broadway and your second Broadway success. Success came early. Where's the thrill once you've done it, once you've made a terrific table so early in your life?

AM: You've got different aims.

MG: Different woods?

AM: Same wood, different aims, to create a different truth. You can't deal the same with a situation as in *The Crucible* or *The Price* or *The American Clock* or *The Archbishop's Ceiling* or the way you deal with *Death of a Salesman*. I have to have a different tone of voice for a different subject. And one to me is as valid as the other.

MG: Aren't you always competing with yourself?

AM: I'm not, in my own mind. I'm doing a different kind of work. The aim is different, the design is different, the sound is different. It's an amazing new adventure. The idea of repeating the same thing would be suicide, although there have been some wonderful artists who have done just that. They've written the same thing again and again.

MG: Who are you thinking of?

AM: Look at Bach: I defy anybody but a real specialist to tell some of those things apart. That's a powerful form — and he's always filling it with high emotion. He invented so much of that form, and once it's invented, it's sufficient.

MG: Do you feel that about writers, too?

AM: There are others. Cheever, I think, was repeating a lot of stuff, but beautifully. You get stylists like Hemingway, with understatement. The same emotions are coming off the same page.

MG: Do you hear your voice through all the plays?

AM: Dimmer or louder, yeah. I think there's one thing to be said about them: they're unmistakably mine. [*laughs*] For good or ill. And I'm happy about that. In other words, I didn't work under such a cover of anonymity that my spirit is not in them. That's one of the reasons I've written so few of them. I really have to be moved to do it. Just to sit down and fill up the pages — I wish sometimes I could do that. I'm convinced some very good work has been done that way. I think some of the Elizabethans did that, more than once. And they stole from one another.

MG: That isn't how you work?

AM: We have different ideas. You know John Golden, who started producing at the turn of the century? I met him, in 1945 maybe. I had written [the novel] *Focus*, and he called me one day and asked if I would be interested in writing for the stage. He had an office on top of his theatre, the John Golden Theatre. He had a barber chair in an anteroom where every morning a barber would come and shave him. On one wall, as big as this, there must be 500 plays. It says "John Golden's Plays." I saw this and I said, "I didn't know you were a playwright." He said, "The plays I produced." I took one down and there it said, "John Golden's Plays, 'Turn to the Right,'" which was one of his big hits, and I look in vain for the author. He said, "You see what we do, we buy the play from the writer, and then we fool around with it. I do a little writing myself. And the director makes some changes and the actors throw in a few things here and there. We give the author $500. You fellas have a much harder job. Everything has to be new." He says in those days — he's talking primarily about pre-1920, "For example, if I had a show in which a woman put a candle in a window so that her long-lost son would see it and find his way home, there must have been 50 plays with a candle waiting for the son to come home." I said, well what did the audience make of this and he says, "They liked it! It was familiar. They knew what the story was going to be."

I started thinking about this, and I thought of the movies. There was a run of Warner Brothers gangster movies. Then RKO made gangster movies. Then MGM. Every major star had to be a gangster for a while. Eddie Robinson, Clark Gable. They were basically the same movie. William Powell and Myrna Loy: very sophisticated movies. Jean Arthur and God knows who — it was the same movie. To be cruder: if you start reading around the Elizabethan times you begin to hear the echoes of one after another. Now come back to the nature of the critic and the audience: God forbid the critic should have heard a line reminiscent of another line in a different work, he's got to raise this not only as a question of the author's originality, but perhaps even his sincerity. This has nothing to do with sincerity. It was a performance. Like a violinist. How sincere is he when he plays some concerto? Who knows? He may just be counting his money when he's doing it. Now it has become much more of a testimonial of some sort. It's almost like the job of a minister. He must be sincere when he delivers a moral lecture.

MG: That's a strange thing, though, the producer owning the playwright.

AM: You know, the Dramatists Guild was created out of this situation. Their first thing was that no writer was permitted under Dramatists Guild rules to sell a play for any amount of money. He could only lease it for that run. I have the results of it now. I sold *All My Sons* in 1948 to a movie company and I didn't realize until recently that they own the rights in perpetuity. This television version — I get nothing out of it. I have the stage rights, but not any film or television rights. That was a hangover from those days. I hear now that royalty terms are such that in effect young writers are giving this work away to producers. We're slowly floating back to the original situation.

AM: Have you seen Fugard lately?

MG: Not recently. He's been in South Africa finishing a play.

AM: I like him. I met a playwright in California who is a friend of my son's. A South African, [Kendrew] Lascelles — and he's been here for fifteen years. He writes plays about the whites of South Africa. There is usually a black or two in the plays. People don't produce them. They're a little verbose, but they could be edited. And I find them terrifying, maybe even a little more than Athol's plays, because I can relate more to the white people. One or two of his short things have been done. He obviously comes from the Boer side of the country.

MG: I thought it was good that in his Nobel prize speech, Elie Wiesel talked about apartheid as well as the Holocaust.

AM: There are a lot more underdogs around these days. I'm glad he did it. It's about time.

MG: I was thinking about your trip with Pinter to Turkey a year or so ago.

AM: I found that in certain select areas, if I go abroad or if I make a statement, sometimes it can have some result, and I feel I should do that. That was one of them. I just met two Turks in Russia. I was in Russia again just a month ago. I had met them in Turkey. One is a Turkish novelist named Yasha Kamal. The other is a composer; his name is unpronounceable. They said that as a consequence of our having gone there, the government released over 1,300 prisoners. Where I think it will do some good, I'll do it.

MG: My reading of that piece you wrote about Turkey was that Pinter prodded you to take even more of a stand — to walk out on that dinner.

AM: I had to. I would have taken a stand, but I wouldn't have done it in that form. I found out later that Pinter might do that at any dinner party.

MG: It doesn't matter if it's political or not?

AM: [*laughs*] He's now very anti-American. He's totally for disarmament in England and wants to drive out American forces. He blames everything on the Americans. But I still like him. He's a wonderful spirit. What happened at that dinner, as I truthfully said, I was glad that he was erupting that way.

MG: That's not something you do?

AM: I can if I'm outraged by something somebody says. If that newspaper columnist [Nazli Ilicak] hadn't maintained that Turkey had a liberal democratic state, I don't think I would have done that. Up to that point, nothing much had happened.

MG: What else makes you angry these days?

AM: Bullshit in general. I wish to God we had a political cabaret. I raised it with Greg Mosher [artistic director of the Lincoln Center theatre company], a place where somebody could write a sketch, have a day of rehearsal, do it, and have tables out there and serve coffee, or get a liquor license. I suppose there are such places. I just don't know of them.

MG: Would you write for it?

AM: Yes! Of course, it's gotten so now that it's hard to satirize politics.

MG: Tell me about your meeting with Gorbachev.

AM: We had been for four days in a place called Issy-Kul. The meeting had been called by the man who is probably the most popular author in the Soviet Union. I had met him a year ago. I never wanted to go back to the Soviet Union, after one of these fucking meetings. It was just a waste of time. As a favor to Harrison Salisbury [an author and a former writer for *The New York Times*] I went. We were supposed to talk about our writings and our personalities. Bill Gaddis, William Gass. The Russians started talking about the black problem in the United States, and another guy was talking about pornography in American culture.

My turn came, and I looked at Harrison who had delivered a most wonderful speech about his youth, how he first got interested in Russia because he was brought up in Minnesota in a Jewish ghetto, with all Russian Jews. Gass talked about his upbringing. And what we're getting from the Russians is boiler plate. So I said, "Look, I'm not going to talk about my life. It's clear to me now that there's not going to be candor. We're talking about our lives. You're talking about something I could have read in *Pravda* yesterday. So why should we come all this distance. I can't tell you guys apart. Every time we ask a question, you all give the same answers. So what is the point? If you're going to talk about the United States, I'm going to talk about Russia," and I pulled out a dossier which PEN had given me at the last moment about this poet that had been in jail for some years. "You want to talk about this woman? Her crime is she wrote some poetry that nobody liked. I had hoped that candor must break out some time. When? It'll be after I am dead. But it will. And at that time there can be some kind of understanding between our two cultures."

At which point, this guy [Chingiz Aitmatov] stood up. I realized I had met him many years ago in New York. He wrote *The Ascent of Mount Fuji*. He had come over for that production. He said, "Look he's right. I agree with him." Months pass and Aitmatov calls me on the telephone. He said, "I'm inviting Fellini and Duerrenmatt and Peter Ustinov, people from all over Europe, and we'll talk about how we're going to get into the third millennium." I said, "I can't come, I'm writing a book." But Harrison Salisbury said, "Look, this invitation has to be coming from the top of the heap, and I think you ought to go."

So I went. And we had an interesting time. Not just writers, scientists too. Fellini sent a wonderful letter. There was no phalanx and there was no attempt to move the discussion over into ideology. I thought that was encouraging. And at the end of the meeting we spent two hours and 40 minutes with Gorbachev. Imagine the President of the United States greeting fifteen intellectuals. He's a tough but contemporary man, sharp as a tack. When I met him, we shook hands and he says, I know all your plays. I was tempted to say, not all, because of the blacklist of the Soviets since 1970. There was a chance we could humanize the relationship. They simply have to modernize the country, which is still half in the 19th century. They have to free up the intellectuals and everyone else in order to create a computerized culture. They lock up the computers at night. After all, a computer is a printing press. There was a moral to the piece that I wrote about this meeting, which is that I think it is changing, but God knows how long it's going to take. And that Gorbachev wants it to change. Why shouldn't he? It doesn't mean he's a humanist because he wants it to change. It's simply intolerable.

MG: With Reagan, this would have been a photo opportunity.

AM: I said that in this piece. Here we're Joe, Moe and Harry, and we wrote this play or this novel. In Russia and in other parts of Europe, the writer is the eyes and ears of the country. They're constantly astonished that a writer here is treated on the same level as an actor.

MG: At best, a celebrity.

AM: A celebrity, that's a very good way of putting it. Gorbachev doesn't give the American ambassador two and a half hours, unless there was some crisis. In Europe, if a guy achieves any distinction in the arts, he's already a philosopher. I had some Chinese to my house once and I had my tractor out. Of course, in China a tractor would serve a commune of 5,000 people. The idea that I could get on that tractor and ride!

AM: I can think of ten stories a week that would make wonderful plays, and never do them.

MG: What's the starting button?

AM: For example, these two plays [*I Can't Remember Any-*

thing and *Clara*]. They're both based on reality in one way or another, and a great affection. That's another thing I've got to have, some kind of love involved. It may be the most circuitous way. I love those two people in the first play.

MG: Are they real people?

AM: They're combinations of people. And the second one likewise. The background is a mixture of two or three backgrounds. The detective is somebody else. But in different ways they were both obsessed with the same thing. It's that kind of confluence of things. In other words, how does one affect the fatefulness of life? Here's a man who inadvertently taught his daughter to be a heroine. Inadvertently he reached his apotheosis through her. That's a wonderful thing.

MG: Have you written before about fathers and daughters?

AM: No, except in *A View from the Bridge,* and that was once removed. I'd love to do more of that. It moves me a lot. You never know where it's going to come out of. Maybe that's why the plays endure. They have to deal with basic human dilemmas.

AM: I saw *The Crucible* in Soviet Georgia years and years ago, and they played it in their historic period. They had these pantaloons with pointy long shoes, and big mustachios. They injected a scene in the play where the whole town is running after John Proctor. The Russians love to have a big turntable, on which they put trees, a tremendous forest, and have a character running through it. It's very scary, a wonderful effect. They do it whenever possible. They would do it in *A Doll's House*, if they could.

There were two revolves, covered with enormous trees, and they worked out a ballet where Proctor was running in between these two revolves, which were turning in opposite directions, with a mob of people. There is no such scene in the play, of course. And indeed it was quite a striking scene. It had nothing to do with anything. They had these guys running with scimitars, real curved Turkish blades. [*laughs*] I'll never forget that. It was like something out of *Alexander Nevsky*. It was quite a way from Salem, Massachusetts. They had a great time doing it, and the audience enjoyed everybody chasing everybody.

After finishing our conversation, we walked through the snow to his studio, a solid-looking, plain structure, hand-made by the playwright-carpenter. Inside, it was unadorned and filled with files, books and papers, a desk and a computer. Clearly it is a workroom in which he feels comfortable. On the wall were several paintings by his daughter Rebecca and a sign, given to him by Dustin Hoffman. It read "Boston. Providence. Route 1," a reference to Willy Loman's journey as a salesman. On the desk were four notebooks, filled with notes and scenes from his play in progress, The Ride Down Mt. Morgan. *All his plays since* Death of a Salesman *had been written here. After showing me around, he opened the door to the terrace adjoining the studio and stepped outside. Facing the snow-filled vista, he seemed to luxuriate in the view and the brisk country air. He took a deep breath. Then, bringing everything down to basics, he said, "This is where I piss."*

January 7, 1987

"The subject was right here. There was never a question in my mind about that"

On December 15, 1986, rehearsals began for I Can't Remember Anything *and* Clara *at Lincoln Center. Miller stopped by artistic director Gregory Mosher's office, took an apple off the table and then sailed into the rehearsal room. He seemed to be on a high. "It's like the day of creation," he said, and added about the actors, "They're about to take it away — and I'm just a bystander." Under Mosher's direction, the actors started reading the plays. Miller watched intently and only occasionally interrupted to offer a comment. Three weeks later on January 7, I met him at the Mitzi Newhouse Theatre, the smaller of the company's two theatres, and we walked to the nearby Ginger Man restaurant for lunch. Wearing a tweed jacket, tall, straight-backed, he had an air of being on top of the world. We entered the restaurant, and he immediately started talking about Geraldine Fitzgerald, Mason Adams and the other actors in his one-acts.*

AM: The tragedy of our theatre hit me all over again when I saw these actors here. In England I have three casts working and you think, what actors, what a fund of actors. I came back here and saw these four people, and I realized that we have actors just as fine. When you see productions like *All My Sons* on television or *The American Clock* in London, it just makes you feel that there's still a reason to do this whole bloody thing. It's very moving to me, apart from the fact that it serves me.

MG: Which play were they doing today?

AM: *I Can't Remember Anything.* Incidentally every time I tell somebody that title, they laugh, thinking I'm making a remark about a title I can't remember. Then they think, jeez that's me, I can't remember anything. I'm afraid the whole country's memory is sliding.

MG: I wonder if we could talk about your autobiography [*Timebends*] again, your reasons for writing it, the problems you had while writing it.

AM: Actually the autobiography is a kind of shuttle form, that is, I might be talking about my young years in Harlem, where I was born, then shoot ahead thirty years, because some theme in Harlem moves me to that. So it's not a consecutive autobiography. If it were, it would probably have to be 5,000 pages. The selectivity is based on the themes that directed my development. I follow those themes rather than dates.

MG: What themes?

AM: One would be the collapse of what seemed to me to be an ordered society, which I was born into in 1915, and continued as far as I knew until 1929 [the year of the Wall Street crash]. Now, that smashing of the society was very important to me as a dramatist because it goes into the forms of my plays. They begin with an equilibrium, either openly or implied, and proceed to tip that equilibrium.

MG: Everything starts out placidly?

AM: You start at dead level, like in *Salesman.* Willy already is in a bad state right at the beginning, but always implied in everything is his reversion to some period when nothing disturbed the equilibrium. This is the basis of all his reveries when the boys were young.

MG: Washing the car, playing football. Was there a point when you were growing up that you felt that your world was ending? Was it the Crash itself?

AM: It wasn't just my father's catastrophe, but suddenly a catastophe of the great leaders of society like J. Pierpont Morgan. The public was very hostile to big business at that moment. The head of the stock market was soon in Sing Sing. Mayor [Jimmy] Walker turned out to be a charming petty crook.

MG: What did it mean in your own family?

AM: First, the denials, which were inevitable. "This was all going to pass" — that was the slogan of the administration, too. "Prosperity is just around the corner." A few people, then some more, began taking to suicide. Then one man — I didn't know him personally, but my parents did — and this was a shocker. People who only a year ago were seemingly solid citizens now were jumping out of buildings or taking gas. The value system collapsed. That vision of the fragility of relationships goes right down into *After the Fall,* and it occurred at a particularly sensitive moment. I was just turning thirteen [the family moved to Brooklyn in 1928], and here I was without leaders anymore, in or out of the house. This was, I think, symptomatic not just of me, but of that whole generation. They did two things: they didn't believe anymore in reassurances, and they believed totally in Roosevelt.

MG: Did that trigger your desire to be an artist?

AM: It's hard to imagine that a whole world shook, and indeed it was literally a world, Europe as well as here. And the only stable area ideologically and spiritually seemed to be the Soviet Union, where there was no unemployment, where there was no collapse. This was the advertised truth. And indeed they were recruiting people in Detroit to come over and build factories and work in the factories. I went through the two concomitant things, as did the whole generation. The main thing to me was that the most solid seeming faces of the society turned out to have no reality. So what did you do? It made you want to search for ultimate values, for things that would not fall apart under pressure. And that I think is the moralistic side of my work.

You begin to believe that the society, as vital and important as it always has been to me, was second to what people carried around in them, what they believed about themselves and about life as far as stability was concerned, and being able to function. The symbolic figure of the Depression was the man sitting in the Automat at eleven o'clock in the morning with his cup of coffee — and he has nowhere to go. He's not starving to death. He's had a job all his life, or a business. He has no appointments, and no foreseeable ones either.

MG: It sounds like an Edward Hopper painting.

AM: It's exactly like out of Hopper. You see, Hopper's work is out of that Crash. It was that sense of stasis, the sense that the damn thing was never going to move again. All these great institutions were gone. There were people who made money in the Depression time but that was a very small minority. They were guys who were able to think in those terms. But I suppose I was typical of that time. The idea of nihilism, of cynicism, was not attractive to me. To most of us at the time — you couldn't afford it. [*laughs*] Everybody was trying to figure out why there were no jobs. You were absorbed in trying to fix the thing. You had to have money to be a nihilist.

You had to say, nothing is going to work, so why should I worry about it? And then dip into your pocket and you got a few dollars — if you had a few dollars. Hemingway had been part of that culture, which said, in effect, to hell with the economy and the political stuff, right through the 1920s. He was basically a Bohemian. In *To Have and Have Not*, it reached him. The line was something like, "One man alone is no goddamn good," meaning that there had to be some kind of organized resistance to this slide. One didn't admit to having one's own nihilism.

MG: Couldn't it have driven you into one of the professions, into medicine, or, perhaps, law?

AM: I had these fantasies from time to time, and they always collapsed because the idea of all that memorization simply floored me. At one point at [the University of] Michigan, history fascinated me. In fact that was the time I first learned about the Salem witchcraft. It was simply a bizarre incident. I had no attitude toward it. I began considering becoming a history teacher. But the appalling amount of boring material — I simply couldn't discipline myself that much. I couldn't discipline myself well enough to become a teacher of anything. I was really groping from one subject to another.

MG: What made you sit down and write a play?

AM: That was my sophomore year at Michigan. At that time, the theatre was the most exciting form. That's where all the action was. I don't recall attaching that much excitement to prose writing. The short story was exciting, novels less so. This was 1933, 1934.

MG: Weren't Hemingway and Fitzgerald coming along then?

AM: They were the great novelists — and Steinbeck came out.

MG: For a young man at that time, deciding to be an artist, the attraction might have been to go off to France, like Hemingway and Fitzgerald.

AM: I knew the subject was here. France was the moon, as far as I was concerned. The subject was right here. There was never a question in my mind about that. It was the most exciting place I could imagine. I had no connections to European culture at all. It literally was a cultural lunar landscape. I gravitated toward the theatre, I think, in part because it seemed to be exciting. The Group Theatre was making the first noises, and there were all sorts of revolutionary things that were going to address the population directly. But I think it's more internal than that. My talent was to write scenes, dialogue. When I tried to write prose, it was the dialogue that became the most persuasive, and the descriptive parts the most laboured. I was aware of that, too. I think that's essentially why I became a playwright. Carried along with it was the feeling that with a play you could change the world.

MG: Why would you think that?

AM: That was the propaganda of the moment, the cultural

notion of these new theatres, especially the Group. Harold Clurman [a founder-director of the Group Theatre] was a great issuer of edicts, papal bulls. And I began to be struck by the great 19th century European playwrights. That reached home quicker than any of the literature, excepting for the Russian novelists. But who could write Russian novels? I was swimming with the given conception. Basically, though, it was my own bent.

MG: The idea that Odets could write about the common man as hero must have been an inspiration.

AM: That's right. Theatre before the Depression, at least so far as my consciousness was concerned, was all make believe. It involved people one would never hope to meet, played by Gladys George or some other lady, or a very handsome leading man. It was also the way the new actors were looking. Nobody could mistake John Garfield for anything but a guy from the block. Or Kazan, when he was an actor. Or Lee Cobb. Or any of them. Morris Carnovsky. They had a sprinkling of Franchot Tone, a little style, that was all.

MG: You wrote eight plays and buried them all.

AM: Well, they got buried. But they helped. I won prizes with them. I was hoping I would write one that would get produced. I was testing the reality of my vision, that I could make somebody else see what I thought I was seeing. Most of the time it didn't work. Partly the reason it didn't work, I'm convinced, is that behind seemingly ordinary stories, I was laboring with some metaphysic, which I was unconscious of, but it was trying to get out, and the metaphysic was a kind of doom. The first time it really showed any aborted expression was a play about Montezuma and Cortez, *The Golden Years*, which I wrote in 1938, 1939.

MG: Looking for turning points in your life: the first was the

Crash; the next was when *All My Sons* was a success?

AM: No. It was winning the awards at Michigan as a playwright. That was the first recognition. The Hopwood Award was judged by outside writers like Susan Glaspell, a number of critics, other playwrights, and it was all done anonymously. The scripts were unsigned. On some objective level, somebody thought I had some ability. It was such a shock. But it turned me around. I realized that I could hope to make a life writing. That was very important.

MG: Your very first play was a straightforward realistic play about your family, and it won a Hopwood prize.

AM: And the Federal Theatre did a production of it for a week in Detroit, and that was the end of it. But it won another prize, the one that Tennessee won, from the Theatre Guild. They gave me $1,250, which was a fortune. The play had several titles. *The Grass Still Grows.* [it was also known as *No Villain* and *They Too Arise*] Another turning point was the failure of my first Broadway play [*The Man Who Had All the Luck*]. The next big turning point was when I decided to write a play, which I would be able honestly to defend every moment of, however long it took to write it. I spent two and a half years on *All My Sons,* with that in mind.

MG: Can you think back to what provoked you to write that play?

AM: Yes. My then mother-in-law who lived in Ohio, a little town called Berea, told me about a young girl during the war who had turned in her father. I don't recall what he did, but it was something with the government selling them defective stuff. It was fairly early in the war and I was very struck by that. It was a shocker. Anyway, that got changed into a boy. At that time I had written seven or eight plays and I wasn't getting any produced. I was getting on to 30, and I knew a lot of young writers who clearly were never going to make any life out of this thing. I didn't want to do that. Then this story hooked me, so I decided I would try to be as remorseless with myself as I could be and be sure that every page was really working.

By this time, I had been taken up by Herman Shumlin, who had produced Lillian Hellman. He was one of the two or three director-producers of any seriousness on Broadway. Of course there was no Off Broadway, so Broadway was where you went. Or nowhere. He read the play and said, "I don't understand it." I thought, what is there not to understand? Kazan and Clurman had just set up a company to produce plays and both of them were offering themselves as directors. Kazan appealed to me more. He seemed more my style. Clurman seemed a little bit remote. And that's how it started. It didn't require a lot of rewriting. I eliminated one long speech.

MG: Even after *All My Sons,* you were not completely convinced of playwriting as a career?

AM: Two weeks after *All My Sons* opened, and after the initial struggle it became rather a success due to [Brooks] Atkinson [drama critic for *The New York Times*], and it won the critics' award [the New York Drama Critics Circle prize for best American play]. I was making $7,000 a week. *All My Sons* was doing very well. I feared I would be torn loose from reality by all this, because I was making more money in a week than I would ever hope to make. Suddenly fame beckoned, and I was resisting. I just felt that's not where I want to be. I just went down to the unemployment agency run by the state. I took the first job they offered, which was in Long Island City, in a box factory. It was terrifying. I'm glad I did it because I reminded myself again that a lot of people were doing that work. They were putting dividers in wooden boxes. Beer bottles were stuck in these dividers. The work was so boring, I couldn't bear it. After a couple of weeks I realized I could do more good to myself and to the human race.

MG: You've written about the rehearsals of *Salesman*, when Lee J. Cobb was lying low...

AM: Lying low? Dying! Dying a slow death.

MG: Then finally one day coming alive.

AM: That was maybe the most single magical moment of my life in the theatre. It was close to two weeks into rehearsal. In those days, you had your first public performance in Philadelphia about three and a half weeks in. Here we were, about half that time. Everybody else in the cast was prepared to perform. They were very quick and eager, and you could barely hear him. He seemed to be totally disconnected from anybody else, walking around looking for something on the floor. We had been calling him the walrus. He would lie there with his flippers spread out, swaying from side to side. Kazan kept saying, "He's finding it." After about twelve days I noticed that Kazan began to say it with far less assurance. And after about fourteen days, he began talking about maybe we have to get somebody else. Who that might be, the appalling idea of having to go out now and start to recast this role with that Philadelphia date staring us in the face...He kept after Cobb, tried to make him come to life. But there was no visible change that I could see.

We were up on the New Amsterdam Roof. I think there were only Kazan and me and Jimmy Proctor [the press agent], and Eddie Kook, from Century Lighting. Lee came to the line in the first scene, "There's more people now. The competition is maddening." And he cried that out. [*laughs*] It was the first time you could really hear him. Nobody among us five or six moved. I thought, he's going to lapse back. Then he went on and played the rest of the show. I was simply elevated. I forgot I was in the theatre. He became a dream figure. I was moved to tears by the wonder of his performance, that a human being could do this. There was no set, of course. I had only the haziest idea of what the set was going to look like. But he peopled that block, that city. You suddenly saw an apartment house.

143

It's indescribable. He created life in front of your eyes — and it never ceased.

MG: Have you ever had a comparable experience with another play?

AM: Never like that. I doubt many people have, if only because not many actors would have been able to have suppressed all this for so long. There literally was no sign of life. You always pray that this is going to happen. Of course, Lee was a great great actor in that part. I don't know if he was in every part, but he certainly was in that.

MG: He never had the career one would have thought he should have had.

AM: I was appalled that after some months, he wanted to leave the play, all because he was being offered Hollywood roles that were, in my opinion, not up to his ankles.

MG: In contrast to Garfield, who had some great roles.

AM: Garfield I understand absolutely. Garfield's career should have gone into movies. He was a romantic lead. Lee was not a romantic lead; he never could be. Why would he do that? It was a sign of success for an actor to go to Hollywood. He was making pretty good money, I think, in that role. Certainly everybody was sending him plays.

MG: I wonder if we could talk about something more personal. How do you deal with Marilyn Monroe in your book?

AM: I deal with Marilyn as a person in my life rather than as a figure in a national dream, because that isn't the way I met her.

MG: How did you meet her?

AM: I was in Hollywood to get a film made about a conflict with the ILA, the longshoreman's union, which was then in a kind of a turmoil. Of course in Hollywood then, they weren't doing pictures like that. Kazan thought that if we both went we might talk Harry Cohn into doing it because he came from the west side waterfront as a boy, and also he was enough of a maverick to try something.

Anyway, we stopped by a Fox movie, which was being directed by Kazan's former film editor, and there was this girl crying in the corner, beautifully dressed, waiting to go on to play a part, a tiny role with Monty Woolley. I think it was *As Young As You Feel*. I never saw the film. She was so striking and so terribly sad that the combination struck me. She had to walk across the floor of a nightclub in the film, and she did that a half a dozen times, and we left. I found out later that her agent and lover Johnny Hyde had just died. I had never known him, and that's where we met. Along with 98 percent of the American people, I had never heard of her.

MG: How long was it before you started going out?

AM: It was about four years. We corresponded once in a while. [*pause*] She was really my wife, and that's the way I deal with her in the book.

MG: That whole period must have been a very traumatic time for you.

AM: The only thing that came out of it so far as my work was concerned was *The Misfits*. Until I got married to Marilyn, I never thought about writing a film at all. I didn't like screenwriting because basically you're not in control of it, unless you're going to be the director. So it was chaotic, complete chaos, because she was very badly ill a lot of the time, as she was for most of her life.

MG: Was she ill when you married her?

AM: She really was, yes. More ill than I knew. I loved her. I thought she was the most wonderful person. I couldn't imagine living without her. If I had not felt that way, I would not have. It just couldn't work, as a lot of things can't. It was a tragic circumstance, not the first and not the last.

Either it kills you — or it doesn't!

MG: Did it change you considerably?

AM: In many ways, sure. It changed my attitude towards acting, toward actors, toward theatre, toward art. I don't any longer consider that any sacrifice is valid for an actor or an actress to make. To be an actor or an actress is a very vulnerable position. Unlike any other artist, you're placing yourself on the line. You can get killed doing that because it's you that's being attacked when it isn't working, as well as you who is being glorified when it is working. To have anything in reserve is the art. Living through it. She had no reserve. Everything she was was up there. She took it too seriously. Any actor or actress I see doing that, I can smell smoke. And I wouldn't have thought that way before. Some of my feelings about it all are in *After the Fall*, because the play was the after-wake of that.

MG: How good an actress was she?

AM: She was a very fine comedienne. Whether she could have done other things I can't say. She had a remarkable oblique and therefore very modern, or shall I say postmodern, attitude toward emotion. Apparently she was both able to feel what she was doing and comment on it at the same time. So that irony made her sexuality funny. That's a great talent. Whether anything like this would have counted for her in a non-comic part you can only judge by *The Misfits*, which was a straightforward attempt to act.

MG: The common theory is that she was spoiled by the Actors Studio, by [Lee] Strasberg forcing her into something that did not come naturally.

AM: I think she was made more dependent rather than less, and in her psychological condition that was bad because she needed to have something to depend upon. The nature of Strasberg's approach was to force his domination rather than to free up somebody to do without him. She's not the only one about whom that could be said, but she was so vulnerable that she couldn't recover from it. She became more and more addicted to that dependency, and therefore that was bad for her. Some of the methodology, I suppose, enabled her to work, but all I saw was that it made her more and more despairing that she could ever rationalize herself into a role. She had a natural gift, and she didn't live long enough to absorb any teaching without crippling that gift. So she was working not only to teach herself but to keep that vitality alive, the native vitality that was untaught and unconscious. To do that in her case turned out to be impossible.

MG: When she died, was it…devastating?

AM: I didn't know anything about her life by that time, at all, but as the world knows now she was suicidal many times in her life. I assumed as everybody did that she had gone over the edge. Slipped over the edge. I can't say that I was absolutely surprised. It was horrible. I was horrified by it. At the same time, I knew that she was playing Russian roulette all her life.

MG: Could she have not been an actress?

AM: That's hard to imagine. She was so beautiful — it would have been incredible that she be anything but that. Especially in those days, the studios were all there was in Los Angeles. In different circumstances, she might have been strengthened by her art. The way it is now, the movies are an exploitation situation.

MG: She was really a creation of that mechanized movie business.

AM: And its victims lie all over the scenery. She's just the most pathetic of them, and the most known. This is the cost of that system of production.

MG: Do you think about her?

AM: Oh, sure. She suffered a lot. It was beyond me or any other human being to alleviate it at all. I tried to do it in *The Misfits*, surrounding her with people who would love her and whom she would respect and admire.

"Tennessee felt his redemption lay in writing. I feel the same way. That's when you're most alive"

We met at Miller's apartment in Manhattan. I had just seen a new play by another talented writer and expressed my disappointment in it. We began talking about playwriting and the difficulty of the profession.

MG: How have you managed to survive as an artist?

AM: I suppose partly I was helped by Europe. I think without that I might have given up. I should add though, I was also helped by the resident theatres in the country, and in Latin America, where my work never ceased to be done. In the last 25 years there has been a steady deterioration of the theatrical system. It had little or nothing to do with me or with any individual. For whatever reasons, it's dried up. A number of theatres are dark. These are the death throes. We're always talking about the thing dying, but I don't think it's ever come to this extremity. There seems to be no visionary move on the part of the commercial managements.

MG: Tennessee Williams did not survive. He kept writing and at a certain point they simply stopped producing his plays.

AM: That of course had to do with his personal existence. I've lived in the country because I love it, but I think it's also because it sustains you to a certain degree. The weeks go by before I know that something has become tremendously important in New York. And then it has vanished. So I'm spared all that wasted energy of thinking that I'm missing something.

MG: But it must be much more than the fact that your plays have continued to be done in Europe and Latin America. There must be something in you, emotionally, that has sustained you through your ups and downs.

AM: It's a part of my personality, as much as breathing, to continue to attempt to project a symbol of what I'm thinking — or feeling. And I do that all the time. It's not just what comes out. I've got innumerable starts that never finished. I can't separate my very nature from the idea of struggling to create some kind of form that works. It goes on all the time.

MG: To project a symbol for what you're thinking?

AM: Yes. Which a play is, after all. Most of the time I don't find it possible to manage to do it. But the impulse is always there. It's almost irrespective of the state of the theatre, the fact that it's not welcoming new work.

MG: Tell me about your later false starts. Have there been many?

AM: Oh, yeah. I'm amazed, myself. I had some notebooks for some years, but they're very spotty because I'd break off writing in them for a while, and then go back to it. But there are long scenes of plays I had totally forgotten I had begun. There must be a minimum of four a year. They would go as long as two acts, or three. I've got one now that I hope I'm going to be able to finish, although I have no assurance of it. *The Ride Down Mt. Morgan.* That must involve work over several years. I'm sure there must be a thousand pages of dialogue. I'm trying to discover what it is that's obsessing me about it, so I could find a solid, central order of events.

MG: What is the play about?

AM: It's a kind of picaresque play. It's basically a comedic idea, but it's really ironical. It involves a male character with three women around him. But beyond that I don't want to talk about it.

I didn't know Tennessee much all his life, even less so his last years, but, I think, for him it was something similar. He felt that his redemption lay in writing. I feel the same way. That's when you're most alive. Your most intensive functioning is because of the fact you have discovered an interplay of forces that seem to answer one another, and the call doesn't go out into the darkness anymore. It seems to respond to itself.

MG: Does it help you to work out personal problems when you write a play?

AM: It's not on that direct a level. You end up with the same personal problems that you ever had. If it were that direct, I would be just the most contented human being in the world. It would be like going to the office and working out my personal problems. A playwright especially — although a novelist does something similar — projects himself into a variety of contending characters. He's got to be in all of them. You can't write a character that is not resonating somewhere in you.

MG: In which of your characters do you find more of yourself?

AM: When Kazan was doing *Salesman*, I overheard him one day telling the actor who was the playing Bernard, the boy next door who becomes a lawyer — "That's Arthur." Kazan made an assumption, which has a reality, that there is something in Bernard, vis-a-vis the Loman sons, which is that Bernard is more conservative, more devoted to surviving.

MG: The one thing about Bernard that always lingers in my mind is that he argued a case before the Supreme Court and doesn't mention it — because he has done it.

AM: And that's one of my other relationships to him. It could be merely that, or it could be anything.

MG: Here's a theory: all the lawyers in your plays are closer to you than the other characters.

151

AM: The main lawyer that I know is Alfieri in *A View from the Bridge.*

MG: I was also thinking of Quentin in *After the Fall.* Someone said to me if you want to know Arthur Miller, read Quentin's lines. Those are the lines that are closest to him — in an emotional if not autobiographical way.

AM: I would say that's valid. It's the one in which I was most directly trying to figure out my relationship to all kinds of moral problems that I thought everybody else faced, as well as myself. The death of love — and the rest of it. And it's the most personal statement that I've made. However, there might be more of me, literally speaking, in Willy Loman. You'd have to be to write him that way. A person who didn't share in some part of his heart some of those characteristics, or at least his joys and sorrows, would never think of writing about them. There would have to be in Shakespeare something of Iago, that ignoble son of a bitch. He would have to have passed through that phase.

MG: People have said that one of the characters closest to Tennessee was Blanche.

AM: I believe that Stanley was part of him, too. It can't be a one for one thing. To me, Willy always was struggling with illusions *toward* rather than away from life. He's trying to assert, in this kind of insane, crazy way he's got, a kind of loving ethos. He really wants the boys to love him, and he wants to love them. He's not a purely aggressive capitalist. If he were, he probably would have succeeded.

MG: The common assessment is that he's a man who has based his entire life on false values.

AM: That's part of it. Yes he has, but the other side and what's moving about him is the embrace of the promise of life, as he was given it.

MG: That's the side you would feel closest to?

AM: Yes. Very much so.

MG: Perhaps one correlation between you and Willy could be this need on his part always to be on the road, selling, doing something, not to retire, not to retreat.

AM: The difference between me and that kind of person is that I'm trying to create something with an intrinsic value. I rely on the grace of time to disclose what that value is when it doesn't appear at the moment the play is finished. For example, I did *The Archbishop's Ceiling* at Kennedy Center in Washington, and stopped it there because it wasn't right. It wasn't correctly cast and I had made foolish revisions. I went back in the 1970s and simply used the original script and disposed of the revisions. Now it's at the RSC. It's fine if it's recognized when it happens. I want to believe that it's there, and it might take five years or ten years, or it might be never.

It's not that my plays are perfect, by any means. But you know there is something holy in a first impulse. That's where the vision is clearest and cleanest, especially in the theatre which is so filled with compromises, necessary ones in terms of casting, for example. Or you're not lucky and you get a director with the wrong kind of sensibility. Or the theatre's too big. Or it's raining that night. There are all these variants that are always there. They were there for Molière, they were there for Shakespeare. They will always be there. You're driven back into a corner where you say, "This is what I meant." Let the variations happen around this, and don't start with a lot of compromises.

MG: It would seem that time has caught up to your plays, except for *After the Fall*. When you brought it back, people still did not recognize it for what it attempted to do.

AM: Well, they recognized it more. There was a larger reception for it. I regard it as a very successful run. I don't think that every play has to have a mass audience.

MG: Is there another play of yours that you think will have its day?

AM: Not really. I wrote a play about Montezuma and Cortez

[*The Golden Years*]. There's a certain amount of purple writing in it because it's written in a kind of archaic verse, a Jacobean form. It turned up at the BBC. They're going to do it on the radio, and I said, "Why do you want to do this?" They said that there are some great parts in this thing and we've got all the actors we want, wonderful stage actors to play these parts. [Ronald Pickup played Montezuma and John Shrapnel played Cortez in the BBC production, November 6, 1987] The play was written originally as a response to Hitler, but the character of Montezuma is a man who cannot decide whether the illusion is real or reality is an illusion. They had a god who, according to the legend, disappeared into the ocean and walked across the water. His symbol was a cross. He was white and he had a beard. It fit the conquistadors perfectly. However, the evidence was that they were raping, killing, stealing and melting down holy gold things and giving out that they were going to take over the empire. With all the evidence he had, he was up against an illusion, or a belief, or a fate, which corresponded to his need to believe that he was the last king of Mexico. The god coming back was an epiphany. This was now his final recognition as the ultimate ruler of the world. The point is: now they say, this is what we're interested in because the whole idea of the illusion is absolutely post-modern.

I read the play again, not knowing if I should even let them do it. I got caught up in it. It's an absolutely marvelous story. Who knows? I wouldn't object to it. They probably have more space for it theatrically over in England. The other plays are best left in the drawer, although now they want to publish them as my early work, and they have an introduction written by a scholar at the University of East Anglia. [*The Golden Years* and *The Man Who Had All the Luck* were published by Methuen in one volume in 1989, with an introduction by Miller and an afterword by Christopher Bigsby, an academic and author]. I don't know if people are forgiving enough. I was learning. They were exercises, in a way.

MG: These were not in your *Collected Plays.*

AM: That was the finished work. The others — God knows I spent a decade writing them. I'd like to write a play again, whether it be *Mt. Morgan* or something else. I was at rehearsal yesterday [for *I Can't Remember Anything* and *Clara*] and I'm a sucker for actors. This group has a kind of depth that I think is marvelous. Kenny McMillan is extraordinary. He can be going in one direction, and it's pretty damn fine but it lacks one thing and the director will say, Kenny, and then he turns on a whole new faucet. The emotional equipment of that man is unbelievable. And [James] Tolkan. They're as good as there are.

MG: Would you ever write a play for McMillan?

AM: It moves one to do that. The theatre's competing with big business. You can't really hope to snare a guy of that accomplishment. Or Geraldine Fitzgerald. She's fantastic. But I assume the next time around, I'll call on one of them and they'll say, oh, gee, I'm going to be nine years on television. The theatre's a fifth wheel. You've got to face that.

MG: What are you learning about those plays by seeing them?

AM: One obvious thing: when you've got two people on the stage for an hour, you've got a lot of talking because there are no entrances or exits and we're not going anywhere. So it can be talking, or it can be a play; it can be a struggle — with stakes. I'm thinking of yesterday where Gerry [Geraldine Fitzgerald] and Mason Adams were just talking and Greg said, "Well, that's very good talking, but you know there's a play going on under this talking." [*laughs*] They looked up in shock, and they went back and they did the play [*slaps his hands*], and that was quite marvelous. I wish I had a film of that happening, because it's the same exact dialogue, the actors are in the same places and they're the same people. You see what one level is, and you see what the other level is. It's very hard to explain that to anybody, unless they saw it. One is absolutely riveting. The other is kind of mildly interesting.

I'm writing the subtext as much as I can, and the words are there to illuminate that. But the tension! How they can keep this up for an hour. Because it goes from one point to another point, and I must say that Greg is a tough nut. I hope he lasts long enough to do that. I'm not sure that I have the energy to start at one o'clock and go to four with one play and then up at four-thirty to eight with something else.

MG: The two plays are linked about memory.

AM: They're both plays about trying not to remember. Memory is the danger, and there are two tactics people take consciously to forget pain. One is obviously more comedic than the other. One is by declaring that one can't remember anything, and the other — *Clara*, the play about the murdered girl — is about attempting to remember, but being prevented by one's own culpability. They're face to face or back to back.

MG: Which approach would you take?

AM: I think I do both of them. I'm quite aware that it's much easier to remember pleasure than it is to remember pain, unless you've got some disease. I feel I do both things, those that make one feel the agonies of guilt and the things you just find yourself bearing.

MG: In the first play, what's the attitude towards memory?

AM: The woman uses her absence of memory as a defiance. She's saying rather defiantly, "I can't remember anything and I'm not going to remember anything — and what's wrong with that?"

MG: Perhaps we could talk about your family, and what your children are doing.

AM: I've got three grandchildren, my son's children. He does film and television production. He does commercials and shows and so on. My daughter Jane lives in New York with

Tom Doyle, who is a sculptor. She has been married to him forever. And Rebecca is my youngest daughter, and she does that sort of thing [*points to a painting on the wall*].

MG: Are you close to them?

AM: Oh, yeah. Unfortunately I don't get out to California enough [where his grandchildren live].

MG: Who are your friends now?

AM: A lot of painters and writers. Cleve [Cleveland] Gray is a very close friend of ours, and Francine [du Plessis Gray, his wife]. They're of all generations. Honor Moore is a good friend. People in the magazine world. Saul Steinberg was an old friend of Inge's. [Alexander] Calder was a very close friend.

MG: What about your old theatre friends?

AM: The ones I knew when I was working a lot in the 1950s are either dead or inactive. The actors of course vanish into space. I know the actors from whatever play I'm on. Some of them are business people, professional types. I have a few friends that keep coming back. I've never had that many friends.

MG: Who reads your plays first when you finish them?

AM: That's an interesting question. I don't know anymore. First of all, it depends on whether it's a play that requires enormous forces. For example, I wouldn't do it, but if I wrote an historical play that needed 25 people in it, I probably would have to go to an Off Broadway institutional theatre of some kind. I can't imagine, quite frankly, a Broadway management wanting to do one of my plays anymore.

MG: I was thinking, when you finished a play who you would show it to — your wife or your agent or a friend?

AM: I guess my agent would be the first. Luis Sanjurjo [who has since died]. He's a wonderful combination of savvy and education. Imagine being able to talk to an agent about something.

157

MG: Who haven't you met that you would like to meet?

AM: I'll tell you the one guy I'm sorry I never met and I could have: Sartre. I have an affinity for him. See, he did a screenplay for *The Crucible* [filmed as *Les Sorcieres de Salem*, or *The Witches of Salem*, with Yves Montand and Simone Signoret]. He wrote some interesting commentary about the theatrical problems in this century. It was very impressive. This was back in the 1950s, I think. He foresaw something — he wasn't referring to television when he said that a play now has to be short and make a single *striking* point. That's a paraphrase. The idea being that the attention span was diminishing — for everything. And he wrote endlessly, one immense essay after another. He had a large library of works. He assumed there was some attention span out there. There were a number of remarks like that which made it seem to me that he had his finger on something about the modern circumstance. Our problem in New York is an economic problem and consequently a way of organizing the audience, but the truth of the matter is that the theatre is facing some kind of unprecedented problem, even in places like Poland, before all this trouble, where truckloads of people were not drawn to the theatre the way they had been.

MG: Does this mean that you're going to write shorter plays — more one-acts?

AM: You know the Greek plays were one-acts, and I kind of like the idea of the form, one smashing explosion. I always have. The play that I've been working on [*The Ride Down Mt. Morgan*] is not that at all. It's a very big multi-scene play, big in terms of length but also in terms of movement.

MG: How do you feel about American novelists?

AM: Phil Roth, I think is a wonderful writer, and he's a good friend, and Bill Styron is a very good friend of mine. And Bill Gaddis and Bill Gass. I can't think of all I like. A man named [Robert] Stone. I thought his last novel was terrific.

MG: Do you read much fiction?

AM: I read a lot. One of the great things about living in the country is that I have a lot of time to do that.

✳

MG: Are there things you've left out of your book [*Timebends*]?

AM: My problem is how to digest stuff. I made eight trips to Europe and Africa as the president of PEN, and in those trips I had to deal with a hundred people who were involved with trying to get writers out of prison. I met one of them in the hall at Lincoln Center yesterday, Wole Soyinka. That would be a book all by itself. Because of those trips, there have been very intimate changes within me of the vision as to what man is about and what is life. When I was in Turkey with Pinter last year, we were within a few hundred miles of the Soviet border, talking with a couple of writers, one of whom was badly tortured. This guy is younger than me but not much. He's obviously a leftist, and he was telling me about the Soviets trying to annex provinces of Turkey that were on the border. This guy suffered as a leftist. His bones were cracked by the Turkish military. He ends up on a beach castigating American imperialism. A refraction of that conversation goes right through my life. It isn't simply a political conversation. The power of alienation — that's what he's talking about. He's got to keep intact his alienation. And the problem in our current time is from what are you going to be alienated? How far? What are the real values that you want to cling to? Truth is a meaningless term now. One is that the United States has armed that dictatorship in Turkey. There are large numbers of arms along the border.

The real menace that he's talking about, that they feel very deeply, is from the enemy of the United States, in whose name he was tortured. That's not politics, it's metaphysics.

MG: And it's also personal.

AM: Absolutely. That harks back to politics in Brooklyn in 1934.

MG: I would think, however, that your readers would be more interested in Brooklyn in 1934 and in Marilyn Monroe and Elia Kazan.

AM: They are. They're all in there. They should be interested in other things, and they'll want to be by the time they finish the book because they'll see the links.

MG: What are you going to call it?

AM: I don't know. I'm going slightly batty. I may end up just calling it *Memoirs*.

MG: Olivier called his book *Confessions of an Actor* because he thought that it might sell more copies.

AM: There were only two confessions; one is Rousseau's, the other is the Christian [St. Augustine]. I don't like that word anyway especially in our time.

MG: The word has other connotations.

AM: These are not confessions anyway. It's not as though I was trying to get into heaven as a result of writing this book. The best I can say is that other people are going to be writing something, and at least I will have my own voice. The fantasizing about everybody is so intense.

MG: So much has been written about you.

AM: A goldmine for some scholar.

MG: You do have some notebooks as stimulus for your memoirs?

AM: Yes, but they're of remarkably little help. After I wrote *Salesman*, we moved. I started to clear out a closet and I saw these notebooks hidden under some junk. I took them out and they were from my college years, which had ended in 1938 and now it was 1950 and I found 20 pages of dialogue about the Loman family. But it was in a totally different form. I had completely forgotten about it.

MG: Were the characters actually the Lomans?

AM: No. They were x and y. I was in that early stage of the thing.

MG: You never know what else might be in your study.

AM: I'm afraid so. I have a secretary up there now filing stuff which is lying in piles and packages. I dread having to look at it.

January 15, 1987

"As always, everything is at stake"

Following our last talk, Miller and I had a brief telephone conversation, dealing with art and politics and clarifying a few questions that had come up.

MG: How do you feel about the relationship between the arts and politics?

AM: Even more so today, the arts to me represent man in his vulnerability, in his natural state, whereas politics is about power. It involves impersonations, masks. But after all the speeches are over, the plays are still there. You can't divorce them from life.

MG: Your quest is for human rights, for writers' rights rather than for anything represented by political parties?

AM: In 1964 when I was head of International PEN, it was important to me that as writers we would no longer be above the battle for our right to be writers. There was terrible pressure to co-opt the writer into the system or to prevent him from making observations about it — here and behind the Iron Curtain. I became far more active in that field.

MG: Doesn't that take away from your writing time?

AM: No. It adds to me, it deepens my feelings. I regard this as the essence of my artistic life.

MG: Why did they call you to appear before the House Un-American Activities Committee?

AM: I was signing left-wing petitions for a hundred years before that. I took public positions which they hated. In

163

1955, I was writing a film about juvenile delinquency. An attack was launched on me by the *New York World Telegram* and the film was closed down. That was the temper of the times.

MG: What effect did that have on you?

AM: It made me very skeptical about easy claims of freedom. If you make waves, you're against pretty powerful people. Life becomes far more real and less vague.

MG: With your opening coming up at Lincoln Center, what's at stake for you?

AM: As always, everything is at stake. But I feel positive. Lincoln Center is a far more relaxed place than it was. It's been through the mill. The burden of being the second Moscow Art Theatre is off it. It's not the new Old Vic or the National Theatre.

MG: You said earlier that you laughed while writing *Death of a Salesman*. Why?

AM: When Willy is talking to his boss, he gives all the reasons why he should be on the road. In the old days, he had respect, people had some regard. "They don't know me anymore," which for a salesman is lethal. It's the cruel irony, it's brutal and in some curious way, it's comical.

October 11, 1996

"You hang around long enough, you don't melt"

Just turned 81, Miller was in the middle of one of his busiest seasons. Nicholas Hytner's passionate film version of The Crucible, *starring Daniel Day-Lewis and Winona Ryder, had opened in New York the previous week to generally favorable reviews.* David Thacker's television film of Broken Glass *was shown in September on* Masterpiece Theatre *on Channel 13, and Thacker's revival of* Death of a Salesman, *starring Alun Armstrong, was opening soon at the Royal National Theatre in London. In June, Miller had travelled to Valdez, Alaska, where he was honored at the Last Frontier Theatre Conference. We met for lunch at Union Square Café. I asked him if he was planning to go to London to see* Death of a Salesman.

AM: I don't think I'm going to go over. I've been on too many airplanes. Rebecca [his daughter, who had become an actress and, later, a film director and married Daniel Day-Lewis] went to California and back. On the way there, there was a three-hour delay, and on the way back here two and a half hours. I worry about the air in the goddamn plane. I understand they're not changing the air as often as they used to, because it costs more money. They use up more fuel. If somebody gets on with tuberculosis, you're breathing that air. I don't like it.

MG: And it takes too long to go by ship.

AM: Anyway I get seasick. [*studies the menu*] For the first time in a long time, I'm looking at a hamburger, I haven't had one in so long, and nobody's watching me.

They've got a very good guy playing Willy at the National Theatre: Alun Armstrong. I was at the Reinhardt seminar in Austria, and David Thacker came with four of the cast, the two boys, the actress playing Linda and Alun Armstrong, and we worked every afternoon in a hotel room. Armstrong has a combination of confrontational naturalism and a style that you can't put your finger on, that's bigger than just standing there being real. I'm dying to go over and see him. I could just take a breath and grind my teeth and get there.

MG: Each *Salesman* is different?

AM: They all are. You get different personalities. They are literally different people. [*pause*] If somebody like Gambon played it...which he could easily do! Luckily the British don't know these accents so they feel free to create them. It's just as well. The only thing they're making clear, I guess, is that it's not English. But Gambon was phenomenal in *A View from the Bridge*. If he played *Salesman*, you could see the difference immediately.

MG: But there's the heart of the play.

AM: They can't change that. [*we order*] I'm going to have a marvelous hamburger. [*to the waiter*: Without telling any-body, put a little bacon in it. Maybe you got a tomato, sliced tomato.] Somebody sent me a little magazine, with all kinds of odds and ends in it. In that magazine is a reprint of an article of 1906 from a doctor telling you what your diet should be. And he says, there is no food value in vegetables, there's some food value in bread, but without butter it isn't worth eating. You can just see these people studying this diet as assiduously as we study these diets now. And they probably all lived about as long as we do. But it was very funny.

MG: When Shaw was asked the secret of a long life, he said it was eating only vegetables and exercising. When Churchill was asked the same question, he said it was smoking three cigars a day and drinking a quart of scotch.

AM: Your genetic inheritance is about 98 percent. The older I get, the more I resemble my father — physically. It's quite obvious. I didn't use to think I did at all. He was totally unathletic and I was always playing one game or another. I thought I was far stronger than he was. I probably was at some point. Not anymore — trying to climb out of a taxicab...!

MG: You turn 81 next week.

AM: The 17th. It all went by, and I'm still here, to my amazement.

MG: And still working.

AM: I am. I was working yesterday on a revision of a play. I've been doing it so long that the routine is there.

MG: Is this the play you've been on the last few years?

AM: No, this is another one. I have a new, new play, which I haven't been able to get back to because I went to Alaska. And that was fun. I caught about twelve salmon in about an hour. They're all in the freezer now. They sent them to me. That trip was fantastic. Have you been there? Don't go except in the warm weather. I was fishing with the head of Prince William Sound. He's the guy that's in charge of the safety regulations after the oil spill [of the Exxon Valdez ship]. We caught some fish and then he leaned out on the side of the boat as we were passing floating ice. He had an ice pick and he chopped pieces of ice off the glacial ice — which is blue ice — and he threw it in the bucket. That ice is probably millenia old. It's been compressed. The Japanese import it. They bring it to Tokyo for their drinks because it makes such great ice cubes. I thought that was just great, leaning over the side of the boat, chopping up some eight-million-year-old ice.

MG: If ice can last that long, perhaps that says something about civilization — and about art.

AM: Eight-million-year-old ice! It doesn't melt.

MG: Can we draw a metaphor from this?

AM: You hang around long enough, you don't melt.

MG: You keep gathering honors.

167

AM: It's lovely, but it's enough already. However, when I was in Alaska they did a production of two one-act plays of mine. Absolutely thrilling! *Elegy for a Lady* and *I Can't Remember Anything.* They did them together, which I've never seen done before. The point was the acting was simply remarkable. A lot of those people came out of Seattle, but they normally work in Anchorage, which was amazing to me because it was a very sophisticated production. I wouldn't have thought that would happen up there. So, it was very pleasant, but it's also an awfully long ride on an airplane.

MG: What do you think of the film of *The Crucible?*

AM: I wrote the script, but I didn't quite believe that it would come off like this as both faithful to the fundamental drift of the play and achieving the so-called moral size of the whole work. It never descended to the melodrama.

MG: In some productions, it becomes melodramatic?

AM: They don't know how to do it. That's a question of the actors' awareness, I think. These people could embrace that element and understand it. Winona was raised on a cooperative hippie farm. I said to her, "That must have been interesting." She said, "It was dreadful." Her father is a writer. And Daniel is the grandson of a poet [Cecil Day-Lewis], and he never had much of a formal education, but his mind is very wide and deep.

MG: I thought he added a real edge to the character that hasn't always been apparent.

AM: I think so.

MG: The danger is that Proctor would seem so heroic.

AM: I hate that. I wrote the thing about a damaged man. That seemed to me to be perfectly clear.

MG: That doesn't always come through in productions.

AM: That's because the easiest thing is to reach for tears and to reach for sympathy. Once you leave that door slightly open, they rush right through it, and it's very difficult to avoid. But Nick [Hytner] was tremendously disciplined that way. He comes out of the theatre: I don't know how many productions he's done of big plays, so this was no special challenge that way. We were really lucky. If I had a different director, he would have probably been tempted by the naturalistic conflicts and simply intensified those, and never arrive at what I really wanted. Nick understood this without any discussion. He said, "Of course that's the way it's got to be."

I tell you I've never had a production in my life on the stage or anywhere without a problem. I kept going like this: I'd say, it's going to blow up, somebody's going to get sick, break a leg. We've got to arrive at some crisis. It never happened. This is the only one. *The Crucible* on Broadway was one crisis after another. Nothing went right. Nothing.

MG: You always liked the Off Broadway production better.

AM: The Off Broadway production had one great thing about it: energy. They weren't as good a cast. We had some wonderful actors in the original Broadway production — Walter Hampden, Arthur Kennedy, Beatrice Straight — but they weren't permitted to act. It was directed by Jed Harris, of whom George Kaufman said, "Everybody has to have Jed Harris at least once, like the measles." On Broadway, it was too studied. It was done like a Mozart sonata. Jed Harris kept reminding the actors they were in a classic play. To him, a classic play meant that nobody faces each other when they speak. It was like some French tragedy, where they stand there and they address the audience. That's no exaggeration. They had to hit marks like they were being photographed. Arthur Kennedy [as Proctor] had to come to a certain point and stop. The woodenness of the whole thing sunk it.

Two years later they did it Off Broadway, and it ran for two years. The spirit is throttled — or it's flying.

MG: One thing the movie has is a dramatic sweep. It was wise to film it on location on Hog Island.

AM: That was a blessing. Whatever tendency there might have been to a static, photographed stage play, you couldn't do it there. The environment kept moving in on you.

MG: How would you compare the Hytner movie to the Yves Montand version, *The Witches of Salem* [*Les Sorcieres de Salem*]?

AM: Fundamentally, that was a photographed stage play. That was Jean-Paul Sartre. I never thought he was very adept at screenwriting [despite his admiration of his other writing]. It was simply this scene and that scene and then the next scene. The idea of really making it a filmic event never happened. The other thing about it which was half amusing: Sartre was a Marxist at the time. He subtly shifted everything so that the rich peasants were persecuting the poor ones. I would say that half of the people who were hanged were large landowners. Also they were all Catholics. I think to the French the idea of a peasant that wasn't a Catholic was beyond belief. So there were crucifixes inside all the houses. The whole thing was an absurdity, but it had some wonderful actors in it. [Mylene] Demongeot [Abigail], Yves Montand [Proctor], Simone Signoret [Elizabeth] — she was marvelous. But he hadn't solved the problem of making a film out of it.

MG: How did the screenplay for the Nick Hytner version compare to the play? I thought the language somehow seemed to be smoother than when spoken on stage.

AM: It is. There were a few changes which I made in order to carry the audience with it. There were a few antique uses of language which were eliminated, or I phrased them differently so that an untutored audience could follow it.

MG: Such as what?

AM: I can't remember. I wrote this thing five years ago. It took close to two years to make the film, from the time that Nick came aboard. Before that, there were three years at least trying to find a director because nobody wanted to do it.

Our hamburgers arrive. He says to the waiter, "He gets the cheese. I get the bacon," then to me, "Just don't tell anybody."

I'd have to look at the script. There's less dialogue than there was in the play because the camera is doing so much of the work. However, I would say all the main confrontations in the play are in the movie, things like when Abigail warns the girls not to tell what they were doing out there in the woods. She's got a couple of long speeches which are the climax of those scenes. And, of course, all of Proctor's stuff. It's basically the play, but so much of it is told through camera action.

MG: I thought Scofield was extraordinary [as Judge Danforth].

AM: He's a fantastic actor. He is probably the greatest actor speaking English. I often thought of all the agonies actors have gone through. He walks on the set and says, where do you want me — and he does it.

MG: With the film of *The Crucible* and *Broken Glass* on television, you've had the English helping you in America. Until now, many Americans haven't seen the English productions of your plays. What do the English bring to your work?

AM: Maybe because of the large amount of work they do on classical plays, there's an assumption that fundamentally a play is a metaphor, that it's not simply a series of actions by characters. It is that, but there was a reason for writing the play that transcends that. The English start with the assumption that the play has a metaphorical life. I think that Americans are far more naturalistic in the way the theatre is approached, and that attitude leads to some very powerful realistic acting, which the English envy.

MG: Is it a false assumption that your work is basically naturalistic?

AM: Which it isn't, and never was. But I don't know how to explain that. The only answer I have is that maybe as a result of doing so many classical plays in the normal course of a director's career or an actor's career, which is a very rare thing in the U.S., the English have taken for granted that the play is there to make some transcendent point, or to set up some transcendent situation. Americans are far more involved simply in behavior, both from the directorial point of view and the actor's point of view. It's not just the English. They sent me a tape of the Swedish production of *The Last Yankee*. On one side of the stage there's this gigantic rose, six feet high — and nothing happens to it. It's just there. There's no dialogue about it. From everything I can make out from this tape: it becomes something that's reverberating in terms of its color and its size, over the action. What's at stake here is life. I don't think anybody here would ever dream of such a thing. That's their interpretation of what it's about. I'm using that as an extreme example of something we would never think of doing. They understood that the Yankee is trying to bring life to his wife, that he is trying to save her from death. That rose has some of that indication.

MG: In the production of *Broken Glass* at the National Theatre in London, the set was angular and distorted, almost surrealistic. The television version is more straightforward.

AM: It's very difficult in film, whether it's television or a movie, to carry off a surreal interpretation of something like that. It would look awkward and imposed, whereas on stage it seemed to me to be perfectly OK.

MG: With *Broken Glass*, do you have any preference — for the American version, the English version or the film?

AM: I thought we had a pretty good production in New York. I also thought there was something in the British production which simply lifted the whole perfomance to a metaphorical statement. I don't know that there was any one element in it, except that the set helped. That was a concrete thing. It was a similar thing with *The Last Yankee* in England. It was played on a stage that looked like it was floating in air. The stage was lit from below, and it looked literally like it was something not quite on the ground. A light was coming out underneath it. There were elements in it that I liked better, but there were also successful elements in our production here. I thought John Heard [in New York] was terrific, probably better than the actor in England.

MG: With *Broken Glass* in London, there was one major difference, both on stage and on film — Henry Goodman.

AM: Yes. How did you feel about him?

MG: He's a wonderful actor. He reminds me a bit of Dustin Hoffman: he always brings an edge to his character.

AM: I hadn't thought of that, but you're absolutely right. The difference is that he's far less sophisticated. Dustin gets involved in all kinds of philosophy.

MG: In contrast to the other characters, there's something underwritten about Gellburg. Goodman caught him.

AM: I think he did. I wonder how it will be received here now on television. You know where it goes on forever? In Germany. Isn't that interesting? It may be that, to the generation there now in the theatre, this is all ancient history, especially about the foreign reaction to Nazism, about which they know very little.

MG: Why is it that the English embrace you for your political consciousness yet they attack Pinter for his — almost on the same ground?

AM: I really don't understand it, excepting they have other playwrights who manifestly have social commitments, like Stoppard does. Maybe it's oversimplifying it, but the English keep producing my plays and they also keep producing Tennessee's plays and O'Neill's plays and a lot of other people's plays that never see the light of day here from one decade to the next. I'm not sure but that a broader audience isn't brought into the theatre by the fact that the National exists, the prices are pretty reasonable and so on and so forth.

✳

MG: In a sweeping statement, Robert Brustein said he defied anyone "to name a single work of art that ever changed anything."

AM: What does he mean by change? I think works of art change the consciousness of people, and their estimate of who they are and what they are and what they stand for. I think that's manifest. All classical literature certainly did it. I think people are always looking for images of themselves and of the life they're leading. If you're going to use the word change in the narrow sense of political change — yes, of course. But I don't know that anyone ever made that claim, except occasionally. When Steinbeck wrote *The Grapes of Wrath*, the Congress at the time was deeply affected by it and actually passed laws dealing with the treatment of those farmers.

MG: Was that a rare case?

AM: I would think that was a rare case. I was also thinking of Mark Twain, who gave America an image of itself, which for good or ill can be said to have changed the country in the sense that without that image it would have probably been a different country, mainly the whole idea of the innocent, forever young American with his simple-minded appreciation of reality as against the complications of life. I think that helped to solidify in the American consciousness what we thought we were. We can go into any war secure in the knowledge that we are doing the right thing, because we didn't feel any guilt about it.

I think Mark Twain's example, which is, of course, an immense example, shows that politics does change — change in the sense that he managed to syncretize in one image what was lying around loose. He seized what was available to him and made it his own, and made it the country's own.

I think plays can suggest to people how to behave, how not to behave, what is acceptable, what is unacceptable. I think, in fact, ~~The Crucible for many~~ people brought the consciousness of what was involved in the McCarthy period. To say you're going to a theatre or a movie house or to read a book and you're one kind of person and you close the book or you leave the theatre and you're totally a different kind of person — that's ridiculous. But there are accretions of change certainly. Culture does affect people.

MG: Today people will see *The Crucible* and think about charges of sexual abuse in school and about the religious right.

AM: Absolutely. Some of them will be hostile to it, but others will not be. A work of art sets up terms of reference, in terms of reality. I think *Salesman* disillusioned a lot of people. It made them aware of what the culture is doing to people.

MG: Athol Fugard had nothing directly to do with the change in South Africa, but he had a great deal to do indirectly with that change.

AM: Absolutely. It's all by indirection. Very few things change people directly, excepting something like a sudden collapse of the whole stock market. Suddenly 30 million unemployed; that'll change them. Revolutions change them.

MG: But works of art don't cause revolutions?

AM: I don't think so. I don't think it works that way. It's far more subtle. We get our images of reality from somewhere, sometimes from newspapers, but after all we're receiving signals at every moment, especially these days, with television telling us how to behave, how not to behave, what's allowed, what's not allowed. These are subtle impulses.

MG: The idea that we can watch a television debate and then immediately get the spin on the debate. We could almost skip the debate and just watch the spin.

175

AM: I did just that the other night with Gore and Kemp [a debate of the candidates for Vice President]. I said to Inge, what are we doing here? I'll read a book. I can write the rest of this show. The canned quality of it is so apparent. There's no spontaneity. Sometimes you hate a guy, but he engages you, makes you listen because he's full of surprises. These guys avoid surprise like the plague. It's the one thing they don't want to happen. If one could spring a surprise on the other, he doesn't know what the response is going to be. It's the opposite of art, and I don't think this particular gang has changed anybody or anything. I don't think it's reached anybody. Maybe a few simpleminded sophomores in some high school. But it's a dead duck.

Driving down from Connecticut this morning, I heard [Bob] Dole [running for President] say, "Trust me." He made one or two remarks. Then he started shouting at the top of his lungs, yelling, "Trust me, trust me," about six times. It was very strange. It was hysterical, as though people around him said, look you've got to drill this into their heads, that they can't trust him but they can trust you. And so he started yelling at the top of his lungs. Inge, who comes from Europe, said, "I've never heard that kind of a tone." It was almost out of control, although he probably thought he was in control.

MG: Are you working on *Timebends* part two?

AM: I thought about it. I could do it.

MG: What has happened to you since then?

AM: That was 1987, 1988. [*thinks*] Well, my house burned. [*laughs*] I was trying to think of something extraordinary. Maybe I've lived a nice quiet life.

MG: What can you tell me about the plays you're writing?

AM: One [*Mr. Peter's Connection*] is a kind of outrageous piece of work. I hope it finishes itself in the next few months. It's very funny. I'm not sure it's a comedy. I have a feeling someone in it is going to die. It's a play taking place between waking and sleeping. That's all I can tell you about it at the moment. It's a curious bite on the world, but I'm far from finished with it. The other thing: I still want to do *The Ride Down Mt. Morgan* in New York. I've been doing some more work on it.

MG: Brustein, of all people, gave it a favorable review.

AM: So I heard. I'm beginning to suspect it. It can't be good. [*laughs*]

MG: The plays come out of your obsessions, out of your life?

AM: My plays come out of some fascination with the character and his story. This new one does too, excepting that our stories have become so fragmented and so discontinuous. Unlike 40 years ago, when I was starting, today in the normal course of his life one single individual can be working on five continents, with people speaking eight different languages, and nobody even notes that it's all remarkable. It's crept up on us. I've got this image, like they used to do in the circus: standing on a ball, which has got the globe on it and we're trying to stay on top of that ball. But that's normal.

AM: You know I interviewed Mandela about three years ago for BBC television. That was an education. I asked him, "Why do I get the feeling of great peacefulness in this place?" Admittedly I come from New York and every other place sounds peaceful. He said that it *is* peaceful. I said, "How do you account for that given the conditions?" This is before the change of regime. He said, "Our people know the country is going to them. There's no reason to get excited. It might happen this year or next year, but it'll happen."

MG: Don't you find it amazing that Mandela spent all those years in prison and survived intact?

AM: I don't understand it. The only clue I got: he really thinks of himself as a chief, in the ancient use of that word. When I met him, he wore a shirt which had a design on it. At a certain point, he said, this is the design of my tribe. It was a beautiful woven thing. I thought, maybe that's what kept him going. There's something kingly about him. Majestic.

MG: What would have happened if you had been put in prison during the McCarthy years?

AM: My own feeling was that we were getting close to that. If I had ended up in a jail cell, maybe I would have written some plays. You get your three meals a day. You might get beaten up occasionally. I rather think the other prisoners would be sympathetic.

MG: Does this mean that, no matter what, you would have written the works you've written?

AM: I have a feeling those plays are my character, and your character is your fate. I used to think that had it been a different social situation in New York when I was coming up I would have written more plays. I was up against an absolutely bottom-line theatre, like everybody else was. After a while, if you get thrown back on your face enough times you say, what am I doing this for? What's the point of all this? Takes a year, two years to write one of these things. Especially when the same play would be played abroad and would be running in twelve different capitals, and not here. Then you begin to wonder, maybe I should be writing in Spanish. Or move to London.

MG: Do you regret any of the plays?

AM: It's like regretting that you lost your hair. It's part of my life. I can't possibly think of not having written one of them, because it was terribly important to me at that moment. I would wish that they had all been accepted. They are, here and there. I have a lot to be grateful for. It's a world theatre now, which it wasn't incidentally until the mid-1950s. I remember when they thought it was remarkable that my plays were done in Europe, not because they were my plays but because they were American plays.

MG: But some plays work better than others. *Death of a Salesman* compared to *Creation of the World.*

AM: Oh, sure. But I don't think of it in terms of regret. I think, was there any way for me to have done that differently? Probably there was, but I can't see it.

MG: Some years ago at a tribute to Harold Clurman at Hunter College, you said Harold wasn't a good director.

AM: No. Harold *needed* a director. Harold was a spieler.

MG: Some spieler.

AM: He was *great* moving actors to express their inner life on stage, but if you're talking about somebody who knew how to stage that wasn't Harold. Of course Kazan used to do Harold's staging when they were at the Group Theatre. Harold would call in Kazan and say, "Gadge, do the traffic." He wasn't interested in that. He was interested in the inner life of those people. That's it.

MG: Harold was a better man, though.

AM: Yes. He did *Incident at Vichy*, and I didn't find any astonishing discoveries on his part. Some of the actors did some interesting work. I loved Harold. He did wonderful work on certain things, like [Carson McCullers's play] *Member of the Wedding.* That was terrific, but that was right up his alley. Very loose structure. It was storytelling, it was very sentimental, which Harold really was. He was very moved to tears by things. But I didn't think of him as being all that great a director.

MG: Still you worked with him.

AM: I used to love being around him. We somehow got it on. If there was a problem, Harold didn't want to hear of it. Problem with a script, problem with an actor: he was a

179

sunshine boy. He wanted life to be fun, happiness. He didn't like nastiness, loud noises.

MG: In contrast, what did you want in a director?

AM: Somebody who would face reality. Harold led the flight away, but it was always with tremendous charm. I used to listen to him talk to the actors. This is one of the great mysteries of life. He'd get finished talking to them and they were inspired and I would say to them, "What do you think he said?" Nobody could repeat anything and then I realized one day, it's music, it's not supposed to be repeated, or repeatable. If you can work that way with a director, with Harold, you could do wonderful things.

In the current issue of the Lincoln Center magazine, they asked for comments about the original Lincoln Center company. Larry Luckinbill described the last gathering of the clan [when it was clear the attempt to establish a repertory company at Lincoln Center had failed]. I wasn't there. Where Gadge [Kazan], Harold, and Bob Whitehead addressed the actors who were now being dismissed, in effect. He describes Harold saying, "Well I've got to get on with things." There was an opportunity there to analyze why an important enterprise had failed. After all it was not a private business. It was a publicly significant enterprise. Not a word. Kazan was loudly proclaiming his right to fail, because of his production of *The Changeling.* Isn't that typical?

Kazan was the reality man. Harold was the dreamer, which was precious. It was terrific. I loved to talk to him. But he couldn't run a candy store. But he wasn't supposed to run a candy store.

When we were trying to cast *All My Sons,* Harold would come in every morning, freshly barbered, looking like Wintergreen for President [in Gershwin's *Of Thee I Sing*]. He was beautifully coiffed. He would come and sit down and have his shoes shined. I would say, "Harold who's going to play these parts?" "Don't worry! We'll get 'em." Of course, it was Kazan who did all this.

MG: Just as I fantasized what it would have been like if Harold had run Lincoln Center, I've also thought what it would have been like if he had been the chief drama critic of the *Times* instead of Walter Kerr during that period. What difference would it have made?

AM: It would have made an immense difference. That was where he belonged, and he could have changed a lot. No question. When I was talking before about theatre as metaphor, Harold was always looking underneath the surface. Very often he left out the surface, so actors would say, what am I supposed to do? "Do it!" But I would rather have it that way, because they were inspired. I miss him. I miss him all the time. I could always stop up there and horse around for a couple of hours. He was trying always to defeat the demon which was the commercialization.

MG: On the other hand, Kerr was committed to the commercial theatre.

AM: He was Mr. Show Business — with some elegance. And he knew a lot. He was knowledgeable and educated. Somebody said to me he was a typical Catholic Jesuit. It was the narrowest use of that art: what he was trying to create. I ran head-on into him. My work was exactly the opposite of everything he thought.

MG: It was your work that he criticized, but on another side, it was also Beckett.

AM: Look, Beckett wasn't writing his plays in order to get laughs and tears. There was a concept behind this, a metaphor behind this. He was really recreating the world as he saw it. That's the last thing you're allowed to do, according to Kerr. Not allowed to do that. He would have accepted Beckett if Beckett had dropped in a few lines indicating that none of this was serious, that they were really waiting for…even if they said, God.

MG: *Sugar Babies* [a vaudeville revue with Mickey Rooney] was one of Kerr's favorite shows.

AM: We were talking before about culture, about Brustein saying art never changes anything. The obverse of that is that here's a guy in a very powerful position, who changed the art with his preconceptions.

MG: In spite of that, the playwrights survived.

AM: Put it the other way. If Harold [Clurman] had been there, it would have changed the public's apprehension of theatre and himself of himself. It's amazing with the situation we have here now and have had for a generation that we still have managed to create. I guess the force of theatre is so powerful that nothing can stop it. But who knows what was destroyed in the bud.

MG: You could ask, do artists survive adversity, or do they thrive *in* adversity?

AM: I can only tell you I never had a critic in my corner in this country — excepting for Brooks Atkinson.

MG: But who has? Playwrights don't have critics in their corner.

AM: [*contemplative*] I guess you're right.

MG: Take Pinter in England. Tynan wasn't in his corner.

AM: That's right.

MG: Except for Tynan and Osborne, and perhaps O'Neill and George Jean Nathan — and even then, not always.

AM: As I look back, I honestly feel that I have nothing to complain about.

MG: But you're always complaining.

AM: Well, yeah, you've got to keep the ball in the air. [*laughs*] But I really don't complain. I don't think I do. All I would want would be that critics, so to speak, illuminate the young, because they are followed so slavishly by them.

AM: By the way, I went to see the David Hare play [*Skylight*]

last week. I was touched by parts of it. Of course I'm crazy about both those actors [Michael Gambon and Lea Williams]. You couldn't do it without Gambon. You wouldn't be able to withstand the screaming. He can take a deep breath, talk in a normal voice and shake the building. Another actor would have to be screaming his head off to get that force. I liked the play, but I didn't feel I had been grabbed by the throat, which is what Hare was trying to do. I'm a great fan of Gambon's. I know him a little bit, after *A View from the Bridge*. In a way, he's better than Olivier was, because Olivier always let you know he was doing this and isn't it wonderful? Gambon can really disappear into a role. When you look back, Olivier was saying, now I'm going to show you how I'm going to do this. He never melted into a role. I don't think he was capable of doing that. He was interpreting the role, a little bit like [Vladimir] Horowitz playing. You always knew what Horowitz was doing; he was in total control.

MG: Gambon is the greater pianist? Who else? Is there an actress you especially admire?

AM: Of course the great one to me: she played the detective in the British series.

MG: Helen Mirren. She and Gambon did *Antony and Cleopatra*. The two of them were great together.

AM: You know, she did two one-act plays of mine in London. She played a whore in one of them. It was hilarious, and so moving. Why don't we create actors like that? I suppose we do with De Niro. He's a great actor.

MG: What young playwrights do you like?

AM: I keep thinking Robbie Baitz [Jon Robin Baitz] is going to come up with something. I think he's got a real talent. Of course, Mamet is there already. There's no doubt about that. Who else? I don't see enough to have an opinion. There was one very funny satire of Tennessee [*For Whom the Southern Belle Tolls*, Christopher Durang's thirty-minute spoof of *The Glass Menagerie*]. That was funny.

MG: Have there been many parodies of your work?

AM: They used to do it years ago. Not any more. I think they wore it out. They usually did *Salesman*. They can do Tennessee because he opens himself to parody. It's just on the verge; they overwrite it a little more...It's going to be interesting to see what happens with the film [*The Crucible*]. It is asking an audience for something they don't normally have to give to a movie. They've got to listen, for one thing, and they've got to feel for people who are very strange. Except now they see all sorts of strange people on screen; they have horns...

MG: As people tend to forget, the events in *The Crucible* really happened.

MG: I was curious about the original titles of your plays. For *All My Sons,* it was *The Sign of the Archer. Salesman* was *Free and Clear.*

AM: That wasn't mine. [*laughs*] In desperation, when we were getting close to going into rehearsal, Kermit Bloomgarden [the producer] went into a panic. He said, "Nobody's going to see a play with death in its title." They actually paid for a poll taken on Broadway, asking people if they would go to see a play called *Death of a Salesman,* and of course nobody would. And so I said, look, I'm not changing this. He said, let me suggest some titles. Be my guest. That was one of them. I said, "You write a play called *Free and Clear*, but that's not this play."

MG: Was there an alternate title for *The Crucible*?

AM: I had a great problem with the title. I remember sitting alone in the old Blue Ribbon restaurant on 44th Street. I was there with this notebook and I must have had twenty titles. I had to have it by the next day, because that's when the ads were starting. I kept reverting to *The Crucible,* and I thought if I say *The Crucible,* they're all going to faint dead away. The great thing was that Jed Harris was a snob, and Kermit Bloomgarden didn't know what a crucible was, and probably 95 percent of the audience didn't either. But simply because most people wouldn't know what it was, Jed said, that's a great title. He connected it with the cross, with crucifixion, which is fine.

MG: But that's not *The Crucible*.

AM: No, but you could make some kind of connection. It was Jed really, because Kermit looked to him for show business. Jed thought it was a usable title.

MG: Why did you choose *The Crucible*?

AM: I wanted something that would indicate literally the burning away of the impurities, which is what the play is doing. There are all kinds of images of fire in these other titles, burning, not of witches, but of the impurities. This seemed to me to put it in one symbolic word.

MG: Albee said about you that your plays and your conscience are "a cold burning force."

AM: [*laughs*] Sounds like coal-burning.

MG: What do you think of Albee's work?

AM: I like *Three Tall Women* a lot. I thought it was a really imaginative use of the theatre, and of his own material. Some of the others seem to me to be fixated on style, on elegance of conception and speech. I always had the feeling he was overly impressed with the British. I had a feeling that the work wasn't coming out of Albee. Now the things that did come out of him, work that genuinely came out of him, like *Virginia Woolf* and *The Zoo Story* and the rest of them were really first class. It's wonderful to see that he's realized himself. That's rare in anybody. He deserves much respect for that.

Poor Tennessee. He had the misfortune of being hooked, in effect, by drugs. He wasn't himself I don't know how many years. He was working on his nerve endings. Albee's a terrific character. I think he's very admirable.

185

MG: Along with you and Pinter, he's been outspoken about human rights.

AM: For some period of time, if a writer got involved with human rights, people would say, why? [*hits the table*] Now if you're not involved, they say, why isn't he involved? The shifts in the culture, the changes in attitudes are remarkable. It all keeps coming around, coming around and going around. At a certain point in the 1950s, T. S. Eliot and that whole crew made it impossible to be talking about a writer having a social awareness. Suddenly, the 1960s came and blew it all away.

July 1, 1998

"Anybody who smears herself with chocolate needs all the support she can get"

Four American performance artists had had their grants revoked by the National Endowment for the Arts for reasons of censorship. Known as the NEA Four, they had taken their case to the United States Supreme Court, which, by a vote of eight to one, ruled against them and upheld a decency test for the awarding of federal grants in the arts. At the center of the argument was Karen Finley, a performance artist who had made her strongest public impression by covering her partly nude body with chocolate to simulate excrement and symbolize the debasement of women. After the Supreme Court ruling, I called several artists for their reactions, among them Arthur Miller, who spoke first of all about his own brush with censorship.

AM: Twice in my life I faced charges of indecency. They were both a long time ago. In 1947, *All My Sons* opened in Boston and the Catholic Church condemned it because of a line: "A man can't be a Jesus in this world." They forbade their members to see the play. When they did that, around the corner was the raunchiest burlesque show of all.

The second time was when the Legion of Decency viewed *The Misfits* before it was released, and demanded certain changes. The main one was the scene in which Marilyn Monroe in a fit of despair walks out of the house and embraces a tree. To them, that represented masturbation.

This is the continuing, age-old argument between decency and the human body. It goes on and on. This time it's especially obnoxious. Certain kinds of art will always be called indecent — and they need support. There we are back where we started. Anyone who smears herself with chocolate needs all the support she can get. If she covered herself in vanilla, they might not have been so outraged.

September 8, 2000

"Sometimes it takes a hundred years, and then you get it right"

In 2000, Miller turned 85. A month before his birthday (on October 17) we met for lunch at the Beach Cafe, a restaurant near his Manhattan apartment. He was having another salutary year, with an acclaimed revival of All My Sons *at the Royal National Theatre and* The Ride Down Mt. Morgan *(starring Patrick Stewart) having moved from the Public Theatre to Broadway.* Mr. Peter's Connection, *which had been a disappointment in its New York run at the Signature Theatre Company, had found a more conducive home at the Almeida Theatre in London. He was working on a new play, which was scheduled to be a part of the Signature's tenth anniversary celebration of its house playwrights. He had just came from the Signature, where he had a round-table discussion with other Signature playwrights, Horton Foote, John Guare, Edward Albee, and Maria Irene Fornes. We walked from his apartment to the restaurant. For the first time I noticed that Miller, who had been bothered by back problems, had a slight stoop.*

AM: At the discussion I said at one point that it's all very well to say that Off Broadway is functioning, but what do you do if you write *The Crucible* and you have a 250-seat theatre with a stage about fourteen feet wide, and you've got to hire eighteen actors and have four sets. Are you settling for a chamber theatre?

MG: You've written a new play for the Signature?

AM: I don't know what to do with it. The play is called *Resurrection Blues*. It's not that it's got a lot of people, but there's something about it that wants to be in a bigger space. At the Signature the play would get diminished, but I'm not sure of that. A terrific designer could conquer a lot of the problems. The stage is quite shallow. Somehow there's a lack of amplitude in that theatre. I may be wrong. Maybe it belongs there.

MG: Is there amplitude in the play?

AM: The play takes place in a place like Colombia. It should feel like you're surrounded with desolate space.

MG: What's it about?

AM: It's about the threat of a return of a messiah. Gradually they all get absolutely terrified that it might be Him.

MG: Where did the play come from?

AM: Well, I spent some time in Colombia, but that's not what the play's about. It's about American commercialism exploiting this whole thing, apart from the value of the Resurrection itself. A lot of the people in the country think this young guy is Him.

MG: Him being Christ?

AM: Yes. It's a repressed peasantry. Gradually the audience — hopefully — will begin to believe it, too. He never appears.

MG: Wise choice.

AM: So we don't have that casting problem. They want to do it at the Almeida. I just had a play there, *Mr. Peter's*, and it's now touring in England. They're building a new building, which won't be ready however until next May. The old theatre would have the same problem as this one, but the new theatre will be a real theatre. They found an enormous bus station which is no longer used, not far from the Almeida, and they're going to transform it into two theatres.

MG: Did you see the Almeida's two evenings of Shakespeare with Ralph Fiennes in the Gainsborough studios?

AM: I saw *Coriolanus*. It was terrific. I don't see how else to do it other than the way they do it. Coriolanus arrives on the scene and he's furious, and he never stops being furious. Jonathan Kent told me that Shakespeare's mother died eight months before that play was produced. He wrote it after her death. The mother in that play is such a force. I wonder if it's connected or not. You could make up a good subtext easily with that information.

So, I'm on the horns of a dilemma. I don't know where to do the new play.

MG: You can't just do it on Broadway?

AM: Nothing's for Broadway! I mean nothing I would ever write would be on Broadway. The only hope to put anything on Broadway would be if it was a big hit somewhere else, and Gerry Schoenfeld [the head of the Shubert Organization] ran over there and exercised his great taste.

MG: In 1996 when we talked about the movie of *The Crucible,* you were discouraged about Broadway, but after that you had revivals there of *Salesman* and *The Price.*

AM: Both of those productions originated someplace else, *The Price* at Williamstown and *Salesman* at the Goodman Theatre in Chicago. It may be that that's the way it is now, for our lifetimes, that Broadway becomes a place for revivals, for near star revivals — excepting that the production of *The Price* was a strange beast. There were no stars in that that anybody would buy tickets for. It was very successful, until the Shubert Organization decided they wanted to put *Copenhagen* in that theatre. So they didn't try to find another theatre.

MG: When Brian Dennehy did *Salesman*, he was not a box office star.

AM: I believe that there is an audience for plays, probably as good an audience as there ever was in my lifetime, but you can't expect people coming in in droves at the prices we're charging. It's really more than anyone can expect. They're going to go to the pure entertainment. When they were doing *The Price* and *The Ride Down Mt. Morgan*, the official price was whatever it was, $60, but most of the tickets were sold for $45. So I said to the powers that be, well you guys believe in a free market, maybe that's the price. If I manufacture an automobile and I want $100,000 for that automobile, you're not going to sell as many as you would if you charged $40,000. They said, "Oh, no, no, no, they'll pay for it." I said, "Well, they ain't gonna." Of course, we're in the hands of the real estate lawyers, and all that crap. It's a hopeless situation. But I think the audience is there.

MG: With *Mt. Morgan*, of course, you had Patrick Stewart, who is a star.

AM: He was a star, but I wonder if he was a theatre star. I don't think the audience connected him with drama; it was the personality.

MG: But you've had a lot of plays on recently.

AM: I personally haven't got any complaint. But what we can't do under these circumstances is to build up a core of mature actors and theatre people who are employed in the theatre. There are a few people, a handful, who are prepared to act in theatre indefinitely, Phil Bosco, people like that. But I think you can count them on one or two hands, at most. So it's a great situation for playwrights who are writing about very young people because young actors don't have families yet. They don't mind getting paid nothing. But if the guy's a mature person with a family, he can't do it, not for very long. It becomes a sort of fifth wheel to the entertainment wagon.

MG: The route you just took with Brian Dennehy and *Salesman* — from the Goodman Theatre to Broadway — is the proper way.

AM: Maybe that's where we are. I resisted believing that for too long. I kept saying there must be a terrific Broadway producer the way there was, who would risk everything on a new show. Of course, I can understand part of it, because it originally cost $40,000 to put *Salesman* on, and if you and your relatives anted up $2,000 apiece you could raise it. But you can't raise a million and a half that way. You've got to get some real hard money.

MG: Tell me about your experience with the revival of *All My Sons* in London. What do they do differently?

AM: Well, for one thing, the set [in the Cottesloe Theatre] is a long lawn, real grass, a big swath of lawn, at one end of which is the facade of the house, the other end of which is lawn furniture. The play is played on the earth. The audience surrounds the play.

MG: But you didn't write it as an outdoor play.

AM: They do go into the backyard. It may be the configuration of that theatre. I don't recall it being that way, but they fixed it up that way. *All My Sons* took place on the back porch and in the backyard. In a normal theatre, the house is upstage, and you have a downstage area, with a little arbor, and that's it. This had a vastness to it; it really was like a Greek play. And it's a small theatre. The audience is around it; they're practically in it, and the impact of that is simply overwhelming. They had an actress, Julie Walters, who played it like a Jewish mother. She comes on and she's already quite lively, filled with a kind of neurotic anxiety. The reasons are not given right away, but as the play proceeds that anxiety gets wilder and wilder and by the end she's like Medea.

MG: Some years ago you talked about the London production of *All My Sons* with Rosemary Harris. You said that in that version, it was clearer from the beginning that the wife knew what her husband had done.

AM: Same thing now. She knows the story. She's trying to control that explosion, because her contribution to the tension is immense. You sometimes don't understand why she is that way. But it very rapidly unravels. I thought it was fantastic. The actors have this dynamic inside them because of the training.

✳

MG: We've talked about your uncle Manny and his connection to *Salesman*.

AM: He was married to my mother's sister. He always fascinated me, as he did everybody. Everybody used to deride him because he told such outlandish stories about himself and about others. He could never tell anything straight. What he said was always adorned with some completely impossible circumstance, like how much he sold in some place. Also his emotional life was very interesting because it was very sexual. He adored his wife in an open way that was not very common. They had been married about 25 years by the time I was conscious of them.

MG: He had two sons?

AM: He had two daughters, too. The eldest was a daughter, and the boys were tucked in the middle. That was the matrix, but it became something else. The dynamics of the play itself took over.

MG: He killed himself.

AM: Yes, he did.

MG: Do you know why?

AM: I don't think anybody knows why somebody commits suicide. By that time, I hardly knew him. I was away. I once figured I spent, total in my life, maybe four or five hours with him, in his presence. But the impression was profound.

MG: We know why Willy killed himself.

AM: Yes, of course, that's a different story. I'm sure he [Manny] would never recognize himself [in Willy]. Nor would any of the family.

MG: He was dead before you wrote the play?

AM: Long before.

MG: Do you remember the point at which you decided to write a play that would take off from him?

AM: While *All My Sons* had been a success, my work generally was far more lyrical than that. As I said, the challenge for me was whether I wanted to be able to beat the realistic theatre, or not. Once *All My Sons* went on, I felt I had a license to do what I really wanted to do, which was deal with time the way I had never seen in theatre. Make things happen simultaneously, which I think is the way we perceive reality. The idea that you're never thinking of only one thing, you're thinking of two things, or more, at the same time. It was then that I began to think of Uncle Manny, because in one sentence he could raise two or three subjects and time periods. He was spread all over the map of his own mind. When I was writing the play, in the very first scene, Willy talks about imagining he was in a different car which he wouldn't have been in for many years. He has his sudden switches from one reality to another — I got very excited about that. It was a way in to where I always wanted to be.

MG: In terms of the subject matter, it conjured up things from your boyhood?

AM: In a way. I invented a lot of that, but it was tinged with my early life in Brooklyn. Basically, it was a feeling of more than the biographical stuff. There was that sense that something marvelous was about to happen. The play, I think, is suffused, oddly enough, with hope. Everybody's full of hope! All the time. As well as dread.

MG: Is that a fair picture of you at that time?

AM: Sure. Anybody who would ask if I had a happy childhood, I would have said, yes, sure, I was doing wonderful things all the time, like dreaming I would be a great ballplayer or a great singer, but I was held back by some mysterious force.

MG: At that point, did the idea of becoming a playwright ever enter your mind?

AM: Not as such. I didn't know what that meant. I didn't think about writing until I was sixteen. Before that, I never took writing seriously. I read a lot, of absolutely every kind, but actually to be a writer — it was simply too marvelous an idea. It was filled with glory. It never crossed my mind. I started to think about being a writer only after I left high school, and I had to go to work in various places. Going to work threw me into contact with all kinds of characters whom I would have loved to have been able to capture. That's when the language became useful. It came out of the experience of being with people and trying to capture them. Before then, I had been in a different culture, where painting was important.

MG: At first, you wrote stories rather than plays.

AM: I started to write descriptions of people in prose. They were never very satisfactory. I couldn't make the people live. It was only when I started to see some theatre. Nazimova was playing *Ghosts* at the Brighton Beach Theatre in Brooklyn, down near Coney Island. Somebody must have put me on to it. I don't remember who. I went down there and I was simply bowled over. Not by anything more than the feeling of having been captured by that event, and taken out of myself and made into a different human being for those three hours. To walk away with those visions in your mind was realer than anything around it; I think that set me off more than anything.

MG: Were you aware of Ibsen then?

AM: I didn't know Ibsen from a hole in the ground. It was a show, that's all. It's after I saw it that I began to go to the library and look up some of the other plays. But that's when the idea arose really — that you could make portraits of people in words, and have them tell stories on stage that were coherent and shocking and wonderful, all with language. It always came out of the people. I was very good with dialect.

MG: You've always felt you were a good mimic.

AM: Yes. I used to believe, and I suppose I still do, that playwriting is an auditory art.

MG: Where movies are visual.

AM: And that's why I've never been comfortable thinking of myself as a movie writer, even though I've done a couple of movies. It's like writing about mutes. At any point, if you can eliminate the word, you move. At least, those were the movies I grew up with. I've seen some pretty good movies that have language. But they're unusual...I just saw August Wilson's play *Jitney*. The language is what's keeping that afloat.

MG: And the people.

AM: Because the language is coming out of those people.

MG: That was his first play, and there was such vitality in it. Anyone should have been able to see that.

AM: You would think so. I enjoyed it. It gets moralistic now and then, but so what? Some of that acting was just terrific. The guy who plays the drunk, the way he moves his body, he hoists himself up out of a chair. It was an imitation of somebody he observed getting himself out of a chair. He'd raise himself up by the cushions and swing his body out.

MG: Have you ever had any black characters in your plays?

AM: Not often, because I never lived with them. I had the nurse in *The Ride Down Mt. Morgan*. It's a very good part. In *The American Clock*, there's a couple. But I would really have to bend a lot of reality.

MG: Even though you're a good mimic, you've held to the people that you really know.

AM: I can do that lingo though. I suppose I would feel like an outsider, a tourist. As a tourist, you always think you're experiencing something. Then when you leave the scene and the natives start to talk, you know that you ain't seen nothin'. It's a little like people writing about Jews who really don't live in that milieu. You know that there's a whole life in there that they never got to. It's simply a limitation, which I respect.

MG: As you say that, you haven't often written about Jews. Some people are Jewish in the plays, but…

AM: I'll tell you: I never saw it as a dramatic issue, for some reason. I suppose it's partly because my father was a completely agnostic person — except he'd show up at the High Holidays for an hour or two to pay his obeisance. But religion played no part in my upbringing and indeed the culture played no part because nobody spoke Yiddish. I often wish they had. I wish I had learned Yiddish. My grandfather, who came from Europe, occasionally lapsed into Yiddish, but they were Germanic cultured, so the ideal was German. That's what they thought they were supposed to be doing. I was in fact surprised later in life at all the Jewish culture there was, which had completely passed me by.

MG: So it's never been a major part of your life.

AM: No, it hasn't.

MG: Whereas Harold Clurman used to go to the Yiddish theatre. That's what he grew up on.

AM: By the time the 1920s came around, most of that feeling of vitality had ebbed. My father loved Jacob Adler, he loved him playing Lear. He used to talk about it all the time.

MG: You didn't see that?

AM: I wish I had, but I was too young. I was still nine, ten. You would never take a kid like that to the theatre. I didn't have that experience.

AM: I miss old Bobby Lewis [the director and teacher, and an early member of the Group Theatre]. He was terrific.

MG: He would say whatever he damned pleased.

AM: He had less bullshit about him than any theatre person. He told it like he saw it. He directed *Brigadoon* and it was a tremendous hit, the first time he had a big commercial hit.

He went off to Europe and enjoyed himself. He came back to check up on the show, and, he said, "The show was dreadful. It was full of holes. The actors were mugging all over the stage. It was horrible. But the audience loved it, because by that time it was something you loved."

MG: That's one of the weaknesses of live theatre: performances change.

AM: When Lee Cobb played *Salesman*, I went back there after about two or three months. The play was a good ten minutes longer. He was pausing all over the stage, and redirecting all the other actors, so that he would be where he could be most effective. An inch below the Group Theatre's philosophy [the idea of a theatre collective serving a social purpose] was [the producer] David Belasco. Many years ago I read that Stanislavsky thought Belasco was the genius. I saw a reprint of a letter that Stanislavsky wrote saying, that's what you've got to see, that's how to do it.

MG: Each to his own genius. Some people thought Jed Harris was a genius.

AM: He may have been before he got to me. Well, Jed thought he was a genius. That's a good start. And he would not stand contradiction on that issue.

MG: Who was a genius in the theatre?

AM: Kazan was for a while. But I wouldn't call him a genius, because a genius has implications of some gift from above.

MG: Harold Clurman thought he was.

AM: Yes. Harold was something special.

MG: I watched him teach some of his classes. He would change the title every year, but it would always be a course in Harold.

AM: Bobby used to imitate Harold at breakfast. He would say, "Harold would look down at a plate and see an orange and try to figure out how to get into it." [*laughs*] Oh God. I love those people. They weren't like everybody else. They were desperate about themselves, but it was overwhelming. It transcended the money.

MG: I remember being with Harold at an ITI [International Theatre Institute] Congress in Stockholm, and we were sailing up the fjords past the greatest scenery in the world and he was talking about the Group Theatre. I said, "Harold, look around you." He said, "I've seen it," and went back talking about the theatre.

AM: Bob Whitehead put him in a car someplace in France. Bob was driving the car through the most gorgeous French countryside. Harold was sitting next to him, saying, "What's the next city?" I suppose some people still love the theatre the way they did. Jim Houghton [head of the Signature Theatre] does. Of course, the Group had a lavish way of expressing everything.

MG: It didn't last too long.

AM: No. How many years? Four, five?

MG: And only one playwright, Clifford Odets. But how important it seemed.

AM: Because it raised ideal issues both theatrical and moral, it was in such contrast to the show shop that Broadway is. What they actually did in terms of the work was so small.

MG: The Actors Studio has lasted longer.

AM: I always felt that was a training ground for television and films, if that.

MG: I recently wrote a piece in the *Times* about who would be considered the greatest actor in the English-speaking world. So many of the candidates were British. The Americans were on a different plateau.

AM: You see, very few, if any, ever kept at it. One shot and then they're off to the movies. Our theatre has been a jumping-off spot for films and now television. When I talk to younger people, they have no vision, good or bad, of a professional theatre where a producer is first of all a passionate figure, and he creates a production with a director, regardless of the size of the damn thing, or the number of characters.

MG: In one of your books of essays, you said that Kazan was not a villain but a victim.

AM: I always felt that. But he won't accept that. He was not forced to do what he did [testify as a friendly witness before the House Un-American Activities Committee]. He did it voluntarily, out of conviction, if anything as an heroic figure against the Left. Somebody said the other day that Kazan should have just stood up before that audience on television [when he was given an honorary award at the Academy Awards ceremony] and said, I'm sorry, I felt I had to do this. It's a kind of tragic pride that he won't. I don't think there was a word said about the House Un-American Activities Committee. What about those guys? When I was called to testify, the Congressman from Pennsylvania [Francis E. Walter] called Joe Rauh my lawyer and said, if I were to agree that Marilyn would take a picture with him, he would call off the hearing. And then he proceeded to behave as though I were a menace to the United States.

Last night I introduced [Vaclav] Havel at a Czech Center ovation to him. The Czechs were making a tribute to [the Secretary of State Madeleine] Albright. They asked me if I would introduce Havel. I didn't have a prepared speech. I said, some memories come back about the 1960s when he and I would have to walk in the street to talk. We were afraid of the microphones in the hotel. I said, I had run across repression myself. After all, my passport was withheld for four and a half years and I couldn't travel. But I'm sure this went by in a fog. I don't think it meant anything. That's what history becomes.

MG: What is the point of history?

AM: I wonder. I've been through a lot of stuff that I don't

correctly remember anymore. If I made notes, or put it in my journal, it's there. But often times I go back over that journal, and I've forgotten half of what I put in.

I was talking to Bill Styron once about the 1950s. Of course, that was when he blossomed. He was in Paris with the *Paris Review* and having a great time. The 1950s that I knew were as far away as if it were happening in China. In *The Creation of the World and Other Business*, God's got a line, "Oh you can say anything, nobody remembers anything." It's practically true. There are a couple of images each generation throws up. Those images may tell some of the story. It's all gone. In the case of *The Crucible*, that stuck, which I'm very happy about. I get letters occasionally from people, schoolteachers mostly, in isolated parts of the country, who run up against the same thing. It never gets in the press. They teach the play because it's their voice. But aside from that, who would be thinking about this? Nobody.

MG: Did you read the Joyce Carol Oates novel, *Blonde* [about Marilyn Monroe and Miller]?

AM: I haven't yet. I mean to do it. It's supposed to be very good. She's a good writer.

MG: But the idea of taking Marilyn Monroe — and your life with her — and using it for fictional purposes, don't you find that offensive?

AM: It's probably just as good a way of preserving it. Look at Shakespeare and those kings. It's through art that the generations converse with one another. I regard the Bible as a work of art, but if anyone met an actual Moses, they would flee.

MG: You're going to be 85 next month. You don't feel your age, do you?

AM: Well, I do because I get sleepier after lunch. I used to eat my lunch and go back to work. Now I eat my lunch and collapse.

MG: You work in the morning?

AM: It's my only hope. I will say that certain changes occur. Sometimes for weeks at a time I get energized in the afternoon, and I'm half asleep in the morning.

MG: Do you sleep well?

AM: Nooo, I don't.

MG: And that's where *Mr. Peter's* came from? Lying awake at night? Is there any other play you're thinking of bringing back?

AM: Well, if we ever dare do it right, *After the Fall* would be something to do. [*pause*] Sometimes it takes a hundred years — and then you get it right.

July 23, 2001

"An unelected politician is of no significance — like an unproduced playwright"

During the Harold Pinter festival at Lincoln Center in July 2001, I moderated a panel of playwrights (Edward Albee, John Guare, and Arthur Miller) speaking about Pinter. Miller focused on Pinter's politics, talking about their shared experiences helping dissidents in repressive countries. He told the story again about his adventure with him at dinner at the home of the United States ambassador to Turkey. Each time that he tells it, he adds new information, this time about an airline losing Pinter's suitcases.

I said that one principal difference between Pinter and the playwrights on the panel was that they were not actors. Miller responded with a long and very amusing story about his acting debut at the University of Michigan. It was a play that took place on a ship, and Miller was supposed to go on board to arrest someone. On opening night, he forgot all his lines. He had to be prompted repeatedly by a fellow actor, who said, "Don't you want to come aboard?," followed by "Don't you want to arrest me?" This was the beginning and the end of Miller's acting career. I told Miller that in his early days in rep, Pinter had once acted in a production of All My Sons. *With a laugh, Miller said, "That's the first I heard of it." I called him the next day to thank him for his participation in the panel and to say how much I — and the audience — enjoyed his stories. He said, "I was just getting started."*

The first major American revival of his first Broadway play, The Man Who Had All the Luck, *had just opened at the*

Williamstown Theatre Festival in Williamstown, Mass. Miller had sat in on rehearsals, and had talked to the director Scott Ellis and the actors. He was going back in several days to see the play onstage. I was planning to see it that weekend. We met for lunch. It was a hot day and Miller was wearing a brightly colored short-sleeve shirt. Looking forward to a full season, Miller was in high spirits — with his play in Williamstown, All My Sons *returning to the National Theatre in London and* The Crucible *(directed by Richard Eyre and starring Liam Neeson) coming back to Broadway. That evening he was going to a public reading of* After the Fall *at the Roundabout Theatre.*

MG: Why do you think *The Man Who Had All the Luck* failed in its first production in 1944?

AM: I'm beginning to understand why. The American theatre then was almost totally naturalistic, in the most prosaic sense of the word. There were some playwrights like Elmer Rice who tried to escape from straight naturalism. But it was a great struggle to get people to accept anything but kitchen sink drama. My play didn't fit the categories.

MG: But what happens onstage really happens.

AM: Yes, but everybody in that play is obsessed with the same thing, how people get lucky or unlucky, how their fates are determined. In any realistic work, you would never find that. It's a fable. I think this is what sunk it. They simply couldn't place it in any category, because it was a reasonably fair production.

MG: Do you think the failure of the play had something too with the fact that it opened during World War II and dealt partly with the shortcomings of capitalism?

AM: I think it was a stylistic problem. I don't think the content had much to do with it. Today, if a character came on stage and said openly, "I don't know why I have everything and everybody else has nothing," that would not be a remarkable statement anymore.

MG: How did it feel watching the play again?

AM: It amuses me a lot because it's so naive — but that's its strength. People may sit there and gasp at some of the naivety, but the play penetrates because it's asking questions everybody asks and can't answer. At one point, I had the character commit suicide. There was a critic on the *Journal-American* named John Anderson. I was of course totally unknown. The play had just closed, and I got a phone call from him. I met him. He said, "You should be writing tragedies. There's a tragic overcast to this whole play, which is very hard to create in the theatre. You really believe in the doom that's gathering over this man's head." Had I more interest in it, I may have well returned to that ending because without striving for it in any way, there is a sense of gathering doom. Maybe it should have ended tragically, but somehow I didn't feel it had earned that.

MG: Did you change anything in the play for this production?

AM: No.

MG: Not even a pause, as Pinter would do?

AM: No. There aren't many pauses in this production. Of course, they have this fabulous automobile [a vintage Marmon was the centerpiece of the set]. It's got a lively unpretentious spirit about it. Underneath it all is a kind of a joke, a joke which is deadly. Just when he's absolutely sure his longed-for retribution is about to happen it turns out he does something right and deflects it. That's when the audience laughs and says, wait until the next time.

MG: The play makes a point about the wages of success — and you wrote it before you had any success.

AM: Right. Of course, that theme is forever in the air in this country.

MG: What if the play had been a success in its time?

AM: I wouldn't have written [the novel] *Focus*. I would have probably gone right back and written another play.

MG: Now when you watch *The Man Who Had All the Luck*, do you think of it as being written by another person?

AM: No, I know where I come in there.

MG: Is there much of you in David Beeves [the protagonist of the play]?

AM: As you'll see, the father-son conflict is underlying the whole thing. When I began writing that, I had no such idea in my mind at all. It just happened. Suddenly I knew how to organize that play. I remember the day, because originally these two guys [David and his brother who wants to be a professional baseball player] were not brothers. They were just friends.

MG: Reading the play, I can see certain connections to *Death of a Salesman*? Were they apparent to you?

AM: I see that now, but not at the time. When I wrote *Salesman*, I wasn't thinking of this at all.

MG: What do you see now?

AM: Well, obviously the two brothers and the father, and the disappointment of the father.

MG: What about the hatred of the girl's father toward David Beeves? That made me think just a bit of the reaction of Eddie Carbone in *A View from the Bridge* to the immigrant who is in love with Eddie's niece.

AM: God knows where that came from. I left it wide open as to why that man hates him that way. That's another element in the fabulous nature of that work. It's just pure hatred. It's basically a hatred of sexuality more than of a person.

MG: Pinter's *Birthday Party* failed first time around, but it soon came back. Here it's taken you 57 years.

AM: The secret is to live long enough to see that happen.

MG: How is the new play [*Resurrection Blues*] going?

AM: It's all done. I'm letting David Esbjornson direct it. I have a meeting with him and Bob Whitehead on Sunday about where to do it. It ought to be done away from the city. There's an experimental side to it. I would just like to see what an audience makes of it, and what I make of it once it's up there. I think it could be very exciting. The theatre here aborts the continuation of the growth of a play. In the old days, in the real old days, you went out of town for four or five weeks. The actors became indoctrinated with the play. A lot of discoveries were made, even if there were no script changes, or very few. It all started to come together. There was time, which you don't have here.

MG: At our panel of playwrights, you told the story about your experience with Pinter in Turkey. Pinter's luggage was lost and he had to borrow your clothes.

AM: He was apoplectic, and he couldn't blame that on the United States because it was a British airline.

MG: So he had to wear your shirts.

AM: He had nothing but what he had on him.

MG: Is there a metaphor there? Pinter putting on your clothes, assuming your cloak, so to speak.

AM: [*laughs*] Maybe. He wore the same suit all week. I gave him a couple of shirts, underwear, socks.

MG: So when he protested at that dinner at the ambassador's house, Pinter was wearing your underwear.

AM: What a pretentious human being that ambassador [Robert Strausz-Hupe] was. He reminded me of Lee Strasberg. Unbelievable! He was 87, or something like that.

MG: He didn't know what was going on in Turkey?

AM: He knew what was going on, but they wanted to prevent Turkey from going left. They didn't much care how that would happen. You see the menace there was the Soviet Union, which was practically as close [to Turkey] as New Jersey [is to New York]. The country was horrendously poor. Then they had that Kurdish problem.

MG: At the panel, you also spoke about the Turkish courts, the fact that one man who was condemned to death was allowed to be free — until it was time for him to be executed.

AM: That was the most surrealistic thing. I also walked around in the center of Istanbul with a writer. We passed a very tall building, a 25-story skyscraper, and he said that was where all the torturing took place — up on some high floor. It was a building such as you would find on Park Avenue.

MG: What was the reaction in Washington to your speech about politics and the art of acting?

AM: There were 25 members of Congress in that audience. That is supposed to be the most prestigious speech of the year, culturally speaking. I think they all came expecting a reassuring literary lecture. You look at the list of the people who had spoken there in the past. I don't think they expected what I had to say. The place was full — a lot of young people, too. It took me over an hour to deliver the speech because they were laughing their heads off. As I was reading it, it occurred to me that if [during the 2000 Presidential campaign] some Democrat, preferably Gore, had just spoken plainly about the way he really felt...

MG: In the speech, you said, if only politicians spoke with "relaxed sincerity."

AM: I think often of FDR, that aristocratic way he had. He'd nail somebody to a wall. Just a happy phrase of some kind, and the guy would never get loose of it.

MG: You said that among Presidents Roosevelt was the best actor, and perhaps Clinton was second best.

AM: FDR was the star. I'll never forget hearing him on the radio. He was building up to his third term [1940, running against Wendell Willkie]. He had three major Congressional enemies, Joe Martin, who was the head of the Congress [Joseph Martin, the minority leader of Congress], a guy named Barton [Bruce Barton] and another one named Fish [Hamilton Fish]. He was speaking in Boston. He would say, we have tried to do — whatever it was — but unfortunately it ran up a wall which was built by Martin, Barton, and Fish [three isolationists who were opposed to giving aid to England]. Then he took another issue: "We tried to pass that one, but unfortunately there was a deep hole dug on the road to progress by Martin, Barton, and Fish." On the second repetition, the crowd took it up. As soon as he said "Martin," the whole damn place said, "Barton and Fish!" He did that about five times. The place was rocking! He walked out of there and he couldn't lose. [The mockery of Martin, Barton and Fish was considered to be crucial in Roosevelt's victory over Willkie, because by inference it linked Willkie with isolationism.]

MG: That's also a playwright's trick: to refrain a motif.

AM: Bob Sherwood [the playwright Robert E. Sherwood] must have written that speech. And Sam Rosenman [Samuel I. Rosenman], a judge who was a very good writer, must have had his hand in it. [they both did, and in Rosenman's book about Roosevelt, he said that when he and Sherwood placed the names, Martin, Barton, and Fish in that rhythmic order, Roosevelt smiled broadly] But the ineptitude of the whole [2000 Presidential] campaign, just dramatically speaking, was agonizing to me. I looked at Gore and I thought, that's just a bad actor. Sinking everything.

MG: And as an actor, Bush was marginally better.

AM: Yes. I saw Bush in Rome on television two days ago, and the camera was coming down at him, which is always dangerous because it foreshortens everything. He wrinkled his brow the way he does when he is in deep thought and he said, "I happen to believe what I believe and I believe that what I believe I believe is true." It was horrifying.

MG: Sounds like Dan Quayle: "A mind is a terrible thing to waste."

AM: I think Quayle was a hair better. After all, until the age of 40, there seemed to be no events worth recording in Bush's life. William Sloane Coffin was the chaplain at Yale when Bush was a student, and of course Yale was jumping with protest. Coffin said Bush was remarkable even at Yale for having not the remotest interest, either pro or against; he went through college six feet off the ground. There were plenty of students there who were opposed to the demonstrations and supported the war. Not him. He was just nowhere, drinking his beer, floating through Yale.

MG: He was "well-liked."

AM: Probably he was affable. And he's the President! He isn't the first, of course. After all, we had a President named Warren Harding, who in a speech said, "Wherever I go, I see people living together in families." That was it; that was his remark. No problem. He sees people living together in families. His really rash statement was, "We must get back to normalcy." It seems that they [the Republicans] really long for a pre-Roosevelt America, a McKinley sort of a place. Who would have the nerve and the insensitivity to put all those oil people in big jobs in Washington? At least they could have gotten some faceless lawyers. It reminds me of the time we opened *The Man Who Had All the Luck* at the Dupont Theatre in Delaware. In that production David was played by an actor [Karl Swenson] who, probably 45 weeks a year, played the lead in any Dupont Cavalcade of America show [on television]. A very nice guy. When we arrived in Delaware to do the show, the head of public relations at Dupont invited us for drinks. The guy's name was Russ Applegate. They were thrilled that their man was on stage. They didn't know he was a Democrat. We were right in the middle of the election campaign. Roosevelt was running against Wilkie. In the course of the conversation, Applegate turned to Swenson and said, "Well, what does the election look like to you people?" He said, "I don't know much about it, but it seems to me that Roosevelt is going to win." There were five or six of them and their wives; they all looked absolutely bowled over. Applegate said, "Really? Nobody we know is voting for him." That was a lesson. That guy was head of public relations for Dupont all over the world. They thought there was no point talking to anybody else.

That's a real poll.

MG: How many Presidents have you met?

AM: I only met Reagan. I met Kennedy for a minute. I was at that famous dinner in Washington with [André] Malraux. That night I had a very close look at LBJ, but he wasn't President yet. There was a line of people waiting to go in to dinner. I saw this man twenty feet away leaning against the wall of this beautiful room. He was wearing a blue tuxedo. I was standing next to Saul Bellow. I said, "Saul, who is that?" He said, "That's the Vice President of the United States." The frustration coming out of that man! He was patently unhappy. I'm sure he felt he should be the guy.

MG: When you won your Kennedy Center Honors, Reagan was President.

AM: What keeps this country going is beyond me. We had congregated in a room in Kennedy Center, waiting for our turn to appear on a balcony. Behind the balcony is this reception room. We're waiting five minutes, ten minutes, suddenly Reagan comes in, walks over to me, says, "Art. I just shook the hands of 130 old ladies. And you know, when they grab your hand, you can't get loose. They've got a grip! So what you've got to do...Hold out your hand." I held out my hand, and he grabbed my hand and pressed his finger down on my wrist. He said, "You press down and then they let go." Another President of the United States!

MG: I thought you were going to say that he said something to you about Marilyn and Hollywood.

AM: No. Now that I see Bush, I think Reagan was a genius. If you look at it from the point of view of his whole life, he had to work himself from nothing. He had to deal with all kinds of people.

MG: In your speech in Washington, you said that Eisenhower was a lot smarter than people knew.

AM: Oh, yes. He was regarded — and it's probably one of the reasons he was selected by Roosevelt to head the invasion

— he was regarded as the intellectual among those generals. Like it or not, running an invasion of that dimension, the diplomacy required to deal with Poles, French, English, everybody with their own vital interests — that takes a lot of doing. Today nobody would know that this country has an intellectual core, probably greater than any in the world — in almost any field.

MG: Except politics.

AM: In government: apes. Harold [Pinter] is always outraged.

MG: When I asked him if he could ever imagine running for public office, he said he couldn't join a political party.

AM: He could join a party, but he would sink it in about a week.

MG: What about you?

AM: I couldn't stand it either. Look, it comes with the territory. A politician has got to get elected. An unelected politician is of no significance — like an unproduced playwright. It doesn't matter what he says. As soon as you concede that, which you have to do, you're in an area which is very untidy. People start smiling when they're not happy. They start laughing when they're not amused. They start weeping when they're not sad. The acting begins. It's very tiring. But that's inevitable. We get such a distorted view of everything through politics. I was just thinking of LBJ. If he had not fallen into the old hubris, vis a vis the Vietnam war, he probably would have been one of the greatest Presidents we've had.

MG: He was a supreme politician and what he did for civil rights was remarkable.

AM: He was exactly the right man to do that. A northerner couldn't have done it. An outright liberal couldn't have done it. A reactionary couldn't have done it. It had to be him — and he did it. And he destroyed himself. Those Greek philosophers knew the whole story. You know LBJ told Harrison Salisbury, "Well, FDR had World War II, Truman had Korea, Wilson had World War I, and I have Vietnam."

MG: Perhaps it's better to have a war in Grenada, as Reagan did.

AM: That was a Reagan kind of war. You know, we spent a week on Grenada not long after that. You can't satirize it. It's so absurd, it's crazy. They went in there to rescue these students; there was a medical school. It consisted of about forty people: surfers, sons of rich Europeans who were too stupid to go to a recognized medical school. The medical school is a hundred yards from the ocean, and there are palm trees. One classroom, and they would have a lecture whenever anybody thought about it. I talked to one of them, an Englishman, he said we never knew what was happening. Suddenly there were all these 'copters coming in. I said, were you ever threatened? He didn't know there was a problem. The thing was totally invented.

MG: It sounds like *Wag the Dog*, that movie with Dustin Hoffman.

AM: *Wag the Dog* is not too far from the possible truth. I hope they [the Republicans] don't do too much damage — especially with the environment. I've been living in the country forever. It's hard to imagine how a slight change in the environment can cause catastrophic damage. I have a beautiful pond on an acre and a half. I had it dredged. Stupidly one year I agreed with a local farmer that he could fertilize the field above the pond. So he laid down some fertilizer. This water was pure enough to drink. I wake up one morning and the whole pond is blooming with algae. I never had algae in that pond in fifteen years I owned it. Why? The fertilizer had leached down and created nitrogen in the water, and made that water putrid. There are situations in which people are dependent on water like that to drink. You only rectify it by letting it wash through. It took six months. Once those changes are made, reversing them takes a long time.

MG: When you acted in that play at the University of Michigan, was that your first and only time as an actor?

AM: That was it!

MG: You missed all your lines.

AM: I missed every cue, lost all the lines — and left the stage.
I'm always amazed at Pinter. Of course, he started out as
an actor. I did act recently. An Israeli director made a film,
which hasn't been released here yet. It has the remotest
connection to a novel of mine called *Homely Girl*. The
film takes place in Israel, and he persuaded me to act as the
father. It's two and half minutes on screen. Of course,
screen acting is a different story: very simple, not the same
problem as coming out on stage — which is like coming
out naked. Some actors are really incredible. You could
give Arthur Kennedy a complicated change — change a
word here, a word there, a pause here — and I would say,
"Aren't you going to write it down?" He would just get up
and do the damn thing as though he had been rehearsing it.
I could never do that. There's a kind of inhibition that most
of us have that actors don't have.

MG: But there's such pressure in that profession.

AM: You can count the number of great actors who become
drunks or terrific neurotics. It's a crazy-making profession.

MG: Some actors get stage fright. Some playwrights do, too.

AM: That's easy. I would, too, excepting I really lost not only
my fear but my hope.

MG: You lost your hope? That's why you keep writing?

AM: Yeah. I just do it because I like to do it. A great success,
and you figure, that's wonderful — for this week. You
know the number of playwrights that have been kings of
the moment, and nobody knows their names anymore. It's
something to keep in mind. I've lived long enough to see
playwrights vanish from the face of the earth. The point is
that theatre is such a creature of fashion, fashion in
thinking, fashion in feeling. For anybody to say, oh this is
forever. I doubt very much whether there are many
productions of Maxwell Anderson's plays being done.
Anywhere. Imagine doing *Winterset*? It's laughable. What

is it about those plays? They turn to vinegar.

MG: But in their time, they were supposed to be timeless.

AM: It's interesting, you can do a play like *The Front Page*, because it had no pretension whatsoever.

MG: And *You Can't Take It With You.*

AM: They are stage pieces.

MG: But in their time they were not considered the best plays.

AM: No. They were the bread of the theatre, not the cake.

MG: But plays like *Winterset* or Archibald MacLeish's *J.B.* are pretentious.

AM: I think that's the answer. They are listening to a voice which is inauthentic.

MG: You said about finding a voice, "My own tendency has been to shift styles according to the nature of my subject. If my approach to playwriting is partly literary I hope it is well hidden."

AM: Well, if you look at *A View from the Bridge,* and the language and the structural approach, and let's say *After the Fall,* or any of the other ones. I've dealt with a fairly wide range of people, from working people to intellectuals. I'm really hearing the way different people speak. It never occurred to me to try to maintain the same voice from play to play.

MG: Pinter went from writing about working-class people to writing about intellectuals, but they all speak with Pinter's voice.

AM: I'm speaking with what I conceive to be their voice. Of course, a large part of Pinter's voice has been that air of menace.

MG: Your humor has often been overlooked. Is that your real voice?

AM: It is, in a way. It's what I enjoy most. The new play [*Resurrection Blues*] is very funny. It's a satirical play.

AM: It sounds academic but there are days when I wonder what the future is for this art. On one hand, it seems that more and more people are interested in it. The published versions of my plays sell more than they ever did. On the other hand, you get the feeling that theatre is being overwhelmed by television and movies. But there's a class thing going on there, I think. The more educated people, of which there are many now, maybe they're the ones keeping the theatre alive.

MG: Perhaps it's a narrow audience.

AM: But if it's a solid narrow audience, that's all right. What percentage of the wide American public buys a successful novel — 100,000? We've got 280 million people in this country, or whatever the hell the number is. We can't look at it from the point of view of those numbers. In some form, theatre is going to continue.

Afterword

The next morning I telephoned Miller. There was a favorable review of *The Man Who Had All the Luck* in *The New York Times*. He seemed pleased but he was restrained in his enthusiasm, perhaps a protective guard raised against the possibility of negative reviews. In any case, the Roundabout Theatre was planning on bringing the production to Broadway in March of 2002. Once again, Miller had come full circle. He seemed genuinely excited by the reading the previous evening of *After the Fall,* with Hilary Swank as Maggie. It was, he said, "wonderful," and now a revival of that play seemed to be in the offing.

That Saturday I went to Williamstown to see *The Man Who Had All the Luck*. Although it was clearly the work of a novice — covering too much time and occasionally embracing melodrama — it was fascinating and certainly deserved its subtitle as "a fable." David Beeves seemed like a Jimmy Stewart character, a nice guy who had all the breaks in life — and that made him question his own ability and even his integrity. The setting was splendidly simple and most of the acting was subtle, especially by Chris O'Donnell as Beeves and Sam Robards as Gus, the mechanical whiz who becomes Beeves's best friend. Robards is a son of Jason Robards (and Lauren Bacall). Watching him, I had a flash of memory of his father at the first day of rehearsal of the original *After the Fall* in 1963. I would guess that Miller had a similar reaction.

Back in New York, I looked up the review of *The Man Who Had All the Luck* in the *Times* in 1944. In his dismissive notice, the critic Lewis Nichols had one point to make, and he made it twice: the play tried but "did not come off — through luck or whatever." No encouragement was given to the playwright. (Later in the season, *The Glass Menagerie* opened, and it was appropriately named the best play by the New York Drama

Critics Circle. Indefensibly, Nichols cast the single ballot for John van Druten's *I Remember Mama*.) Briefly discouraged, Miller took a sidestep into fiction, and then, of course, returned to the stage with *All My Sons* and *Death of a Salesman*. A major playwright was airborne. It was not luck that made Arthur Miller. He persisted and eventually ingrained himself permanently in the American — and the world — consciousness, and he has remained creative into the 21st century.

Acknowledgements

This series of books, *Conversations with Pinter*, *Conversations with Stoppard*, *Conversations with (and about) Beckett* and *Conversations with Miller*, began with Nick Hern, and I am grateful for his encouragement and his editing. My wife Ann is, as always, my first and best adviser and editor. Thanks also to our son Ethan and his wife Susan Baldomar, especially for their interest in Miller. Others who have been helpful are my agent Owen Laster; Carol Coburn at *The New York Times* in New York, and Pamela Kent in the *Times* London bureau. I want to acknowledge various actors and directors who have led me to a greater understanding of Miller's plays: Ulu Grosbard, Rose Gregorio, Dustin Hoffman, John Malkovich, Michael Gambon, Alan Ayckbourn, and James Houghton at the Signature Theatre Company; to those who have spoken to me about Miller over the years, including Harold Clurman, Edward Albee, Harold Pinter, and Martha Clarke — and also the other playwrights who took part in the panel on politics, Athol Fugard, David Mamet, and Wallace Shawn. Some of the material in this book, including excerpts from that panel, appeared in different form in *The New York Times*.* My thanks, too, to Inge Morath and, of course, most of all, to Arthur Miller.

Index to Miller's Work